# PRAYING FOR AMERICA

## DUTCH SHEETS

**Regal**

From Gospel Light
Ventura, California, U.S.A.

Published by Regal Books
Gospel Light
Ventura, California, U.S.A.
Printed in the U.S.A.

Cover Design and Interior by Robert Williams

**Library of Congress Cataloging-in-Publication Data**
Sheets, Dutch.
    Praying for America/Dutch Sheets.
      p. cm.
    Includes bibliographical references.
    ISBN 0-8307-2895-3
      1. United States—Religion—1960 2. Christianity and culture—United States. 3. Christian life—United States. I. Title.

BR526.S53 2001
277.3'083—dc21                                                                    2001048314

1  2  3  4  5  6  7  8  9  10  11  12  13  14  15  /  09  08  07  06  05  04  03  02  01

Rights for publishing this book in other languages are contracted by Gospel Literature International (GLINT). GLINT also provides technical help for the adaptation, translation and publishing of Bible study resources and books in scores of languages worldwide. For further information, contact GLINT, P.O. Box 4060, Ontario, CA 91761-1003, U.S.A. You may also send e-mail to Glintint@aol.com, or visit their website at www.glint.org.

# CONTENTS

# A Biblical Response to the Terrorist Attacks on America

(FOR THE PURPOSE OF PRAYER AND EVANGELISM)

As we all observed and mourned the results of the September 11, 2001, terrorist attacks on America, my conviction was and still is, *The response of the Body of Christ and the way in which we pray could very well determine whether our nation turns toward God or away from Him.* Sorrow can lead either to bitterness, which perpetuates greater defilement (see Heb. 12:15), or to repentance, resulting in salvation (see 2 Cor. 7:10). Measured, accurate and biblical responses from those of us representing God are critical responses in such crises.

# How Should We Define Such Events?

Great caution should be exercised in using the word "judgment" to *define* these events. Many Christians understand that America has been experiencing a degree of judgment for some time—sin has wages (see Rom. 6:23). But most biblical judgment is the inevitable built-in consequence of sin, not the direct hand of God. He didn't pronounce curses after Adam and Eve's fall because He was an angry God who loves to curse sinners. He did so because of the inherent results of their actions. And He did it while covering their nakedness and promising redemption— a redemption involving great sacrificial love on His part—the incarnation and death of His Son (see Gen. 3:15).

Rather than the direct hand of God, judgments are often simply the result of forfeiting God's favor and protection. Jonah 2:8 (*NIV*) tells us: "Those who cling to worthless idols forfeit the grace that could be theirs."

A careful and compassionate explanation of reaping (or the consequences of sin and of turning from God) should be our definition of the events. I would advise not even using the term "judgment," because the world will probably not hear anything else we say. Other pertinent Scriptures that could be used to explain the fruit of sin and the forfeiting of God's protection are

Psalm 127:1-2: "Unless the LORD builds the house, they labor in vain who build it; unless the LORD guards the city, the watchman keeps awake in vain. It is vain for you to rise up early, to retire late, to eat the bread of painful labors; for He gives to His beloved even in his sleep."

Proverbs 14:34: "Righteousness exalts a nation, but sin is a disgrace to any people."

Proverbs 28:13: "He who conceals his transgressions will not prosper, but he who confesses and forsakes them will find compassion."

Isaiah 59:1-2: "Behold, the LORD's hand is not so short that it cannot save; neither is His ear so dull that it cannot hear. But your iniquities have made a separation between you and your God, and your sins have hidden His face from you, so that He does not hear."

Luke 13:34-35: "O Jerusalem, Jerusalem, the city that kills the prophets and stones those sent to her! How often I wanted to gather your children together, just as a hen gathers her brood under her wings, and you would not have it! Behold, your house is left to you desolate; and I say to you, you shall not see Me until the time comes when you say, 'Blessed is He who comes in the name of the LORD!'"

Luke 19:41-44: "And when He approached, He saw the city and wept over it, saying, "If you had known in this day, even you, the things which make for peace! But now they have been hidden from your eyes. For the days shall come upon you when your enemies will throw up a bank before you, and surround you, and hem you in on every side, and will level you to the ground and your children within you, and they will not leave in you one stone upon another, because you did not recognize the time of your visitation."

## WHAT SHOULD BE OUR MESSAGE?

Our *message* must be one of carefully balanced *grace* and *truth* (see John 1:17). God's desire is always to forgive and redeem, not to destroy. Our gospel includes—in addition to the incarnation, death and resurrection of Jesus—two other very important messages: repentance from sin, and grace to the repentant. Christ came for the sick, not the healthy; He came to seek and save the lost, not the found. "For God so loved the world that He gave His only begotten Son. . . . For God did not send the Son into the world to judge the world, but that the world should be saved through Him" (John 3:16-17).

This message of grace need not leave out the consequences of sin; but as it is shared, it must be laced with hope and with God's merciful heart. His desire is to *turn* us from our sin, not *destroy* us for it (see 2 Chron. 7:14). He is "slow to anger and abundant in lovingkindness" (Ps. 86:15). At times He actually announced judgments through tears (see Luke 19:41-44); the Scriptures are clear that He takes no pleasure in the judgment of the wicked (see Ezek. 18:23-32).

God forgave a harlot named Rahab and then gave her a prominent place in Israel's history and a part of the lineage leading to Christ, as the great-great-grandmother of King David. He was willing to spare Sodom; He did spare Nineveh when that city repented. And on another occasion He unsuccessfully sought for an intercessor, so He could spare Israel (see Ezek. 22:30-31).

So, yes, our message must call sinners to repentance—we cannot compromise truth—but God's heart of compassion, mercy and grace *must* fill the message with hope. "Return to Me, and I will return to you" (Mal. 3:7) should be the heart of our message. The result of the returning will be healing and restoration.

## WHAT SHOULD BE OUR ATTITUDE?

Rather than one of harshly announcing judgment, our attitude must be one of compassion and mourning. Like Jeremiah and

Christ Himself, we must be able to explain the results of sin through heartfelt tears (see Lam. 1:16; 2:11; 3:48-49; Luke 19:41-44). Too often the world perceives our attitude toward the consequences of others' sins—whether the death of an abortionist or of a homosexual through AIDS—as callous or even smug gladness. Satan is an expert at distorting the perception of Christ and the Church in the eyes of the world. We must be wiser than he and make certain the Christ we reveal—the One who loves sinners—is accurate.

We must also be quick to acknowledge our responsibility in the condition of America:

- Some immature leaders, including prophets immature in their calling, have brought forth only harshness and condemnation in their attempts to call the nation to repentance. This turns the hearts of unbelievers *away from* God.
- On the other hand, many pastors and caregivers have overemphasized mercy and grace, refusing to call individuals to biblical accountability.
- The Church in America as a whole has preached a "What's in it for me?" humanistic gospel, leaving out the message of taking up our cross and laying down our lives. This has produced great compromise and lukewarmness in the Body of Christ.
- Many of us have failed to truly care for and minister to the poor and hurting and in general have lacked genuine compassion.
- We in the Church have decried materialism, greed and the love of money as a great part of the problem in America, while fewer than 20 percent of us even tithe, let alone give sacrificial offerings. Our hypocrisy contributes to the problem.

• We have failed to pray as we should for government leaders and the lost.

We must acknowledge that judgment begins at our house (see 1 Pet. 4:17) and do our share of the repenting.

## How Should We Pray?

How can we pray effectively for the nation at such a time?

1. Repent for our (the Church's) role described in the points regarding responsibility. Pray that many in the Church see this need for humility and repentance.
2. Pray that the Church is able to respond to such a crisis with great wisdom—a proper blend of grace and truth—and that neither unwise messengers nor the enemy can distort God's heart.
3. Ask for a turning of our nation back to God—that a revelation of our great need would penetrate the heart of our nation. Believe that God can do this. We have already heard reports of this turning in our nation: prayer happened in the rotunda of the Capitol; a restaurant owner—upon hearing of the tragic events at the World Trade Center and the Pentagon—called out to his patrons to stop eating as they needed to join together in prayer; in the Washington, D.C., area students spontaneously fell to their knees wherever they were—in their classes, on their campuses—crying out to God in prayer.
4. Ask for God's mercy to triumph over judgment (see James 2:13).
5. Pray that our president and other government leaders move with great wisdom and make sound decisions.

Pray that the president would be so visited by God that he would unashamedly and publicly repent, pray and call the nation back to God.

6. Pray for comfort in our nation, but also pray that it would be accompanied with a true recognition of our great spiritual need.

7. Forgive those who have wronged us, yet pray for justice (not revenge) to evildoers. These two things—forgiveness and justice—are not contradictory (see Matt. 7:1; Luke 6:37; Rom. 13:4).

8. Continue to pray for salvation to come to the Muslim world.

# IS THERE NOT A CAUSE?

He stood like a titan on the battlefield. His presence mortified the ranks of the armies of Israel. He was called the shock trooper.[1] He would have made Shaquille O'Neal and his "Shaq Attack" look like preschool stuff. Standing "six cubits and a span" (1 Sam. 17:4), somewhere near 9½ feet tall, Goliath must have looked surreal to the Israelites. Twice each day—80 times in all—this demonized gargantuan Philistine cursed the God of Abraham and caused Israelite warriors to cower in fear.

Yes, Goliath was a shocking giant with a shocking challenge—send out a man to fight me (see 1 Sam. 17:8-10). But still more shocking to David, the young shepherd, was the fact that no one had accepted his challenge. After all, more was at stake than just this one battle. The Philistines, Israel's archenemy, were determined to conquer the people of God and eradicate them from the land. This was winner take all!

Perhaps this is what young David was thinking when he answered his brother's mocking cynicism toward him—and announced he was going to fight the giant—with the question, "Is there not a cause?" (1 Sam. 17:29, *KJV*). What a loaded question! And one, as we shall see, that we in America must ask ourselves at this moment in history.

*There are some causes more important than life itself,* David was implying. *Don't talk to me about how terrifying, imposing or indestructible this giant seems. There is a cause bigger than he is and greater than any potential cost.*

What was the cause David spoke of? It was no less than the survival of the nation Israel:

- their freedom was at stake;
- the well-being of wives and children hung in the balance;
- homes and possessions were on the line;
- the blood shed to purchase their freedom by those gone before was about to be trampled underfoot;
- and, possibly, the very purposes of God through Abraham were in jeopardy!

Don't read that last one too quickly—it's loaded with significance. This challenge was about more than one nation against another; it was more than just a squabble over a few square miles of dirt. The freedoms and destiny of one nation, although very significant, cannot compare to the bigger cause hidden in this drama. The literal purposes of God on the earth were at stake! God's covenant with Abraham and the Israelites was to establish a Messianic line, an entry point for God Himself to enter Earth's fallen race and save the world. No wonder Satan fought Israel so fervently. Eternity for millions of people was at stake. Companionship for God and a Bride for His Son were on the line. The integrity and vindication of a God who promised to redeem fallen humanity were at risk. And the recompense due the destroyer was a part of this plan.

Yes, there was a cause!

Was David aware of this? Perhaps not all of it, but something in him realized this was about more than just Israel's well-being. God was being "taunted" (v. 45). Goliath "cursed David *by his gods*" (v. 43, emphasis added), revealing the deeper and more subtle plot unfolding on this ancient battlefield.

Thinking of this greater cause, David, lover of God, responded with the stated goal "that all the earth may know that there is a God in Israel, and that all this assembly may know that the LORD does not deliver by sword or by spear; for the battle is the LORD's and He will give you into our hands" (1 Sam. 17:46-47).

Clearly, David understood that God's purpose and reputation were at stake! Yes, there was a cause worth fighting for. And fight he did. He rocked and shocked the shock trooper and then took off his head. History was made and the cause was saved. Cause-minded people do that—they create history and save causes.

# GOD'S LOVE FOR AMERICA

This book isn't really about Israel, David or Goliath. This is a book about another nation—America—and her important purpose in the plan of God, as well as today's demonically inspired giants of shocking proportions that are trying to oppose her destiny. *And it's about whether or not there are a sufficient number of cause-minded "Davids" today who see things clearly enough and believe in the cause passionately enough to become history-making, destiny-preserving giant killers.*

We've had heroes of this nature before in our nation. I was recently inspired afresh as I reread *The Light and the Glory*, the masterful work that so clearly outlines God's plan and destiny for America. This book also overwhelmingly reveals the allegiance and dependence our founding fathers had toward God. They were God-believing, God-fearing and, as the following quote illustrates, they were warriors . . . they were giant killers.

> As the Revolutionary War was about to begin, Captain John Parker called out to the seventy-odd Minutemen hastily forming a line on the Lexington green. "Stand your ground! Don't fire unless fired upon. But if they want to have a war, let it begin here!"[2]

We need not make that final statement; our war has already begun. Though certainly a battle of a different kind—"we wrestle not against flesh and blood" (Eph. 6:12, *KJV*)—ours will be no less intense. And as with David and Goliath, and also the American Revolution, spiritual freedoms, the destiny of a nation and the purposes of God on the earth are at stake. Are there enough spiritual American heroes today with the necessary passion to pay the price? We will soon know, for we are in a window of opportunity that many, myself included, do not believe will last long.

Another of our national forefathers, Patrick Henry, in a passionate plea to his fellow Americans to fight for the cause of freedom, declared, "I know not what course others may take but as for me, give me liberty or give me death." Henry and our other predecessors considered natural freedom as a cause worth fighting, and even dying, for. Our battle involves the *spiritual* freedom and *eternal* destiny of a nation and millions of people. Is that not a cause worth fighting, even dying, for? And, as in Israel, what about the distortion of God's reputation? Is He not taunted daily in our land, cursed in the name of false gods? For those who know and love Him, there is a cause.

## THE FIGHT FOR GOD'S REPUTATION

I recently read Tom Brokaw's book *The Greatest Generation*, which chronicles the enormous struggle and price paid by the World War II generation of Americans. I was very moved by their selfless heroism and tenacious determination to defeat the demonized giants of their day and preserve the cause of freedom on the earth. More than 292,000 Americans were killed in battle and more than 1.7 million were wounded in this war.[3] Like those Allied heroes, we're facing our own D day. Are there thousands of spiritual soldiers today who will storm our Normandy—the gates of hell—laying it all on the line for a righteous freedom cause? Is not our eternal cause as noble, our cost as worthy?

Am I being overdramatic in making such shocking comparisons and assertions? "Come on, Sheets," I can almost hear some say. "Is the destiny of America really at stake? Does the eternal well-being of millions actually hang in the balance? Is God's reputation being maligned?" Without a doubt! Consider the following facts and assertions. They will make my point.

Certainly, as with Israel and Philistia, God's reputation as the one true and living God is at risk in this nation. America is looked to more than any other nation as an example of what it means to be a Christian nation. But our sin now mocks and reproaches Him, not to mention the false picture it gives to the world of what a "nation under God" should look like. God's reputation is being affected. Our motto "In God We Trust" is now no more than a faith-filled statement of hope, clung to by a remnant determined to make it a reality again.

The God who was pushed from our hearts by the giants of pride, materialism, humanism and pleasure was inevitably expelled from our schools, government and the core of American life. The shocking results were predictable: We have now killed over 40 million babies in what is supposed to be their safe haven of nourishment and development. *And this is praised!*

> **Our motto "In God We Trust" is now no more than a faith-filled statement of hope, clung to by a remnant determined to make it a reality again.**

Protecting animals and trees is considered noble and praiseworthy, but fighting for the unborn is deemed a sign of intolerance and bigotry.

Isaiah prophesied this lunacy: "The people will be oppressed, every one by another and every one by his neighbor; the child will be insolent toward the elder, and *the base toward the honorable*" (Isa. 3:5, *NKJV*, emphasis added). We now even crush the skull and suck the life from a half-born baby and then finish the birth process of the now murdered corpse. This procedure, called partial-birth abortion, is "justified" because the feet aren't yet out of the womb? *Human beings*—mothers, fathers, national leaders, even some in the Church—fight for this "right" and consider it noble freedom-fighting. Like the Israelites, we have cowered from the giants, and their winner-take-all lust is insatiably feeding on our very offspring, our flesh and blood. The holocaust still continues.

Shocking? I'd say so! Where did we go wrong? How did the love of life die and give way to such insanity? We kill what we once would have died for. God help us!

Our children now follow our disregard for life, killing one another and themselves. Consider these alarming statistics in America:

- Over 2,000 teenagers a year commit suicide—6 each day.
- 3,610 teenagers are assaulted and 80 raped *every day*. That's 1,317,650 assaults and 29,200 rapes annually. (Remember, this only counts teenagers.) Are you shocked yet?
- 1,106 teenage girls get abortions every day—403,690 each year. Is there not a cause?
- 4,219 teens per day contract sexually transmitted diseases (1.5 million each year). These diseases, many of them causing sterility and some even death, have become another ploy of Satan to wipe out a generation.[4]

Is it any wonder that school massacres like those at Santana High School (Santee, California); Columbine High School (Littleton, Colorado); Thurston High School (Springfield, Maryland); Westside Middle School (Jonesboro, Arkansas); Heath High School (West Paducah, Kentucky); and Pearl High School (Pearl, Mississippi) take place now in America? Life is cheap. Greed and selfishness are in; sacrifice is out. Authority is mocked, while rebellion and violence are extolled by our so-called role models and heroes. "If it feels good, do it" is more than an overused cliché—it is a terrifying reality.

When it is suggested that allowing God back into our schools might help, smugness and defiant arrogance are often the responses of those who so desperately want Him out.

Since losing their niece Rachel Joy Scott in the Columbine massacre, John and Debbie Phillips have reached out to thousands of teenagers with their Life Choices Presents program. This multimedia, antiviolence motivational presentation, geared to public middle and high schools, has received overwhelming response from students and teachers alike. Unfortunately, the administration at Santana High School in Santee, California, declined the Phillipses's oft-repeated attempts to bring their program into the school in 2000 and early 2001. In John's opinion the attitude conveyed by the school administration was "Hey, we don't need a program like that here at our school—it would never happen here." Yet on March 5, 2001, a 15-year-old boy firing a gun in Santana High School killed 2 students and wounded 13 others. I guess some would rather run the risk of students shooting one another than to entertain the possibility that we might be wrong about the need to invite God back into our schools. Things are shockingly out of control.

The assault on the American family is now in full force. The bumper sticker that reads "Focus on your own damn family" is considered witty in my city of Colorado Springs, which is home to Focus on the Family. Satan's attack on the home is bearing fruit. During the twentieth century, the divorce rate rose 700 percent in America. Thirteen million children under the age of 18 are growing up with one or both parents away from home. Seventy percent of all juveniles in state reform institutions come from fatherless homes.[5] And we wonder why our young people grow so disillusioned and dysfunctional. *They're simply reaping what we've sown.*

Other signs point to our true condition. We are a nation of addicts and lawless rebels. The United States is the single largest market on the earth for illegal drugs, and it leads the world in the export of pornography. Does that shock and appall you? I hope so.

We cannot build prisons fast enough to hold the criminals. The phrase "The land of the free and the home of the brave" is now an oxymoron at best. We are rich in goods and poor in character—powerful without and weak and self-destructive within. Our wealth and power have anesthetized us to our true condition—we're bleeding to death internally while continuing to party on.

And speaking of partying, our former president did a lot of it. The true moral condition of America was illustrated to its greatest degree when this president had sexual relations with a young intern in the Oval Office and then lied about it under oath. As a whole, Americans are pretty forgiving, which is a good thing; but the bad thing about this situation was that they simply didn't care in the first place. As one of the president's spokesmen so eloquently put it, "It's the economy, stupid."

And that, of course, is the sad truth. As long as we Americans are prospering and can feed our insatiable appetites for pleasure and things, we really don't care about much else. Recent public-opinion surveys show that moral decay now rates as one of our top-rated national problems. But those surveys also show that fewer than one out of every five adults personally rates moral deterioration to be of such importance. Few Americans accept personal responsibility for any degree of the moral dilemma of the United States.[6]

And what of the Church in America, God's messenger, His salt and light for this mess? Many Christian leaders think we're doing a pretty good job of reaching our nation. Do the facts support this? Consider the following:

- 1998 brought about no change in the percentage of adults who are born-again Christians.[7]
- When compared to statistics for 1991, church attendance and Bible reading are at lower levels of involvement.[8] (My note: This means we have actually lost ground.)

- Six out of 10 Americans (61 percent) agreed "the Holy Spirit is a symbol of God's presence or power but is not a living entity."[9]
- A majority of all born-again Christians also reject the existence of the Holy Spirit (55 percent).[10] (My note: Of those who *profess* to be born again.)[11]
- One out of every five born-again Christians believes that the Bible contains errors.[12]
- Rather than following Jesus' exhortation to be in the world but not of it, today's Christians seem to thirst for the opposite reality: to be inseparable from the world, while somehow retaining the aura of devout followers of Christ.[13]
- Only 44 percent of born-again Christians are very certain of the absoluteness of moral truth.[14]

As I have already said, most of the Church thinks we're doing a pretty good job. I've been nearly stoned by spiritual leaders in my city for implying that we're not getting the job done. But the alarming truth is that Colorado Springs now has over 300 gangs, leads the nation in single mothers and ranks close to the top in suicide and child abuse. My city, like yours, is in trouble.

Things are shockingly out of control, and the giants in the land are mocking us. Every part of American society is screaming for some cause-minded people. Our condition is like what the cause-minded Nehemiah observed about his nation—our walls are down, our gates burned (see Neh. 1:3); Hosea's description of ancient Israel also provides an accurate description of America's attitude toward God today—that is, we sow the wind and reap the whirlwind (see Hos. 8:7).

Don McLean wrote a song for America in the '70s, one of the most popular songs of all time, in fact. A notable and favorite line of this song, "American Pie," is "the day the music died."

McLean was more prophetic than he knew. We, like Israel of old, hung our harps on the willow tree a long time ago (see Ps. 137:2). Our songs of "Amazing Grace" and "America the Beautiful" died with our souls.

## An Accurate Diagnosis

I don't like to write these things and I'm sure you don't enjoy reading them. But the first step toward healing is an accurate diagnosis. I fear that most of us Americans are like the man Mark Twain wrote of. Describing a fight he was obviously losing, the man said, "Thrusting my nose firmly between his teeth, I threw him heavily to the ground on top of me." Sounds like good ol' American optimism.

We have become the proverbial frogs in the kettle. And like the band on the *RMS Titanic*, we continue playing while the ship is sinking. Please don't misjudge me. As you will see, I have hope for America. But for hope and optimism to be legitimate, they must exist in the light of reality. Otherwise, they are nothing more than denial. The truth is, *we are* the causeless army of Israel, convincing ourselves that if we wait long enough, the shocking giants of the land will go away and leave us alone.

This will never happen! Satan has no intention of letting up in his relentless assault on America. Positive change in America won't come because the giants give up. It will come when a people of passion, like David, rise to the challenge and meet the enemy in battle. It is not too late, but things are critical.

In their book *Is It Real When It Doesn't Work?* Doug Murren and Barb Shurin recount:

Toward the end of the nineteenth century, Swedish chemist Alfred Nobel awoke one morning to read his own obituary in the local newspaper:

> Alfred Nobel, the inventor of dynamite, who died yesterday, devised a way for more people to be killed in a war than ever before, and he died a very rich man.

Actually, it was Alfred's older brother who had died; a newspaper reporter had bungled the epitaph.

But the account had a profound effect on Nobel. He decided he wanted to be known for something other than developing the means to kill people efficiently and for amassing a fortune in the process. So he initiated the Nobel Prize, the award for scientists and writers who foster peace. Nobel said, "Every man ought to have the chance to correct his epitaph in midstream and write a new one."[15]

God is giving us a chance to rewrite our epitaph. If written now, it would read "Weighed in the Balance and Found Wanting" or "The Shock Trooper Won."

But God is gracious and merciful! He forgives sinners and heals nations. He is slow to anger, abounding in loving-kindness, and to the Davids with a cause He gives anointings to slay giants. Listen to these comforting verses:

> "Yet even now," declares the LORD, "return to Me with all your heart, and with fasting, weeping, and mourning; and rend your heart and not your garments. Now return to the LORD your God, for He is gracious and compassionate, slow to anger, abounding in lovingkindness, and relenting of evil. Who knows whether He will not turn and relent, and leave a blessing behind Him?" (Joel 2:12-14).

Come, let us return to the LORD. For He has torn us, but He will heal us; He has wounded us, but He will bandage us. He will revive us after two days; He will raise us up on the third day that we may live before Him. So let us know, let us press on to know the LORD. His going forth is as certain as the dawn; and He will come to us like the rain, like the spring rain watering the earth (Hos. 6:1-3).

Fear not, for you will not be put to shame; neither feel humiliated, for you will not be disgraced; but you will forget the shame of your youth, and the reproach of your widowhood you will remember no more (Isa. 54:4).

Instead of your shame you will have a double portion, and instead of humiliation they will shout for joy over their portion. Therefore they will possess a double portion in their land (Isa. 61:7).

Repentance of sin, turning back to God and true revival are America's *only* hope. Will it happen? Will we see the fulfillment of these hope-filled promises? If there are enough cause-minded giant killers we will. Look at more of Patrick Henry's famous speech and allow its passion to saturate your soul:

If we mean not basely to abandon the noble struggle in which we have been so long engaged, and which we have pledged ourselves never to abandon until the glorious object of our contest shall be obtained—we must fight! I repeat it, sir, we must fight! An appeal to arms [our weapons will be spiritual] and to the God of hosts is all that is left us! They tell us, sir, that we are weak; unable to cope with so formidable an adversary. But when shall we be stronger? Will it be the next week, or the next year? Shall we gather strength by irresolution and inaction?

Shall we acquire the means of effectual resistance by lying supinely on our backs and hugging the delusive phantom of hope, until our enemies shall have bound us hand and foot? Sir, we are not weak if we make a proper use of those means which the God of nature hath placed in our power. There is a just God who presides over the destinies of nations. The battle, sir, is not to the strong alone; it is to the vigilant, the active, the brave.

The war is inevitable—and let it come! I repeat, sir, let it come.

It is in vain, sir, to extenuate the matter. Gentlemen may cry, "Peace, peace"—but there is no peace. The war is actually begun! Our brethren are already in the field! Why stand we here idle? What is it that gentlemen wish? What would they have? Is life so dear, or peace so sweet, as to be purchased at the price of chains and slavery? Forbid it, Almighty God!

I know not what course others may take but as for me, give me liberty or give me death.[16]

Sounds like a man with a cause. Sounds like one who loved freedom and America. And it sounds like a man who believed in God's destiny for America!

Like Henry and the other early patriots, we must fight! Our enemies are spiritual and so are our weapons; but the war is just as real and the stakes are even more important—the soul of a nation and the cause of Christ on Earth.

Greatness is found when American character and American courage overcome American challenges. When Lewis Morris of New York was about to sign the Declaration of Independence, his brother advised against it, warning he would lose all his property. Morris, a plain-spoken founder, responded . . . "Damn the consequences, give me the pen." That is the eloquence of American action.[17]

## CHAPTER TWO

# HISTORY MAKERS

I was smitten recently by the thought: *We can either watch history being made or we can make it.* I want to be a history maker. I love the song entitled "History Maker," sung by Delirious? (a Christian worship band from England). It was written for such a time as this, when God is calling history makers to step forward in America and around the world.

On my last birthday, a friend gave me a beautiful pen inscribed with the words "History Maker." Will I really become one? We'll know in 20 or 30 years. But I can assure you of one thing—I'm going to spend my life investing in the process.

A recent survey asked adults what they would ask a god or supreme being if they could get a direct and immediate answer. Nineteen percent said they would want to know whether or not they would have life after death. Sixteen percent would ask, "Why do bad things happen?" Six percent would ask how long they would live, and 12 percent weren't sure what they would ask. An astounding 34 percent wanted to know, "What's my purpose here?"[1] I was amazed; this question won by a landslide. And yet I shouldn't have been surprised. Everyone needs and wants to have a purpose. Our purpose is to write history for God.

## MAKING HISTORY IS POWERFUL

The thought of *making* history is powerful, but *past* history is also very important. Karl Marx said, "If I can steal their history, I can steal their country." Roots are powerful; foundations matter. In the previous chapter, we quoted the question David asked before he faced Goliath: "Is there not a cause?" Interestingly, the Hebrew word used for "cause" (*zod*) also means "history." Therefore, David may have also been asking his brother and his fellow Israelites, "Is there not a history?"

What would he have meant by such a question? Perhaps he was asking, "Don't we have a history worth believing in and fighting for?" Or thinking of his fellow Israelites' unbelief, maybe David was asserting, "Is there not a history of faithfulness from our God that brings enough confidence to face this giant? What about Abraham and the promises made to him? Didn't God come through with Isaac and with the land He promised? And what about the Exodus with all of its miracles, followed by Joshua, Caleb and the victory over the giants they conquered? Come on, guys, isn't there enough of a history with God to bring the needed courage to face this giant? *We have history on our side.*"

He also had a personal history testifying to God's faithfulness. He told Saul the story of the lion and the bear that tried to steal his sheep.

Your servant has killed both the lion and the bear; and this uncircumcised Philistine will be like one of them, since he has taunted the armies of the living God. . . . The LORD who delivered me from the paw of the lion and from the paw of the bear, He will deliver me from the hand of this Philistine (1 Sam. 17:36-37).

History is powerful! It can be built upon. It gives both reason to fear and reason to believe.

But David wasn't only a history *rememberer*; he was a history *maker*. Is it possible that he was thinking about the future when he asked the question, "Is there not a cause?" In fact, *Are we not writing history today?* may have been the essence of the question.

Then David said to the Philistine, "You come to me with a sword, a spear, and a javelin, but I come to you in the name of the LORD of hosts, the God of the armies of Israel, whom you have taunted. This day the LORD will deliver you up into my hands, and I will strike you down . . . *that all the earth may know that there is a God in Israel*" (1 Sam. 17:45-46, emphasis added).

What we do today will have a profound effect upon tomorrow. God's future reputation and Israel's legacy were being determined by the decisions they were making. What a cause!

## History Is on Our Side

And what of we Christian Americans today who face the giants in our land? Do we have history on our side? "Yes!" scream the Pilgrims, our founding fathers and early settlers. Knowing that Marx was correct when he spoke of a country's history, there are anti-God forces trying to rewrite American history. But we have a godly heritage in this nation that cannot be denied.

As the founding fathers of America declared their independence from England, they also acknowledged their dependence upon God. Very much aware that He was the author of their existence, they relied on God to provide the wisdom and leadership necessary to create and maintain a new nation.

The Declaration of Independence has four clear references to God and concludes with these words:

> For the support of this declaration, with a firm reliance on the protection of the Divine Providence, we mutually pledge to each other our lives, our fortunes and our sacred honor.[2]

After signing the Declaration, some wept. Others, like Witherspoon, bowed their heads in prayer. Samuel Adams rose and stated, "We have this day restored the Sovereign, to Whom alone men ought to be obedient. He reigns in heaven and . . . from the rising to the setting sun, may His Kingdom come."[3]

Now that's some history to build on!

These men weren't in any way confused about whether or not they wanted God to be a part of this nation. Nor was George Washington, who recorded his prayers in a journal, as evidenced by the following entry:

> Let my heart, therefore, gracious God, be so affected with the glory and majesty of (Thine honor) that I may not do mine own works, but wait on Thee, and discharge those weighty duties which Thou requirest of me. . . .
>
> O most glorious God . . . I acknowledge and confess my faults; in the weak and imperfect performance of the duties of this day. I have called on Thee for pardon and

forgiveness of sins, but so coldly and carelessly that my prayers are become my sin and stand in need of pardon. I have heard Thy holy word, but with such deadness of spirit that I have been an unprofitable and forgetful hearer. . . . But, O God, who art rich in mercy and plenteous in redemption, mark not, I beseech Thee, what I have done amiss; remember that I am but dust, and remit my transgressions, negligences and ignorances, and cover them all with the absolute obedience of Thy dear Son, that those sacrifices (of sin, praise and thanksgiving) which I have offered may be accepted by Thee, in and for the sacrifice of Jesus Christ offered upon the Cross for me.

Direct my thoughts, words and work, wash away my sins in the immaculate Blood of the Lamb, and purge my heart by Thy Holy Spirit . . . daily frame me more and more into the likeness of Thy Son, Jesus Christ.

Thou gavest Thy Son to die for me; and hast given me assurance of salvation, upon my repentance and sincerely endeavoring to conform my life to His holy precepts and example.[4]

These are the words of one who knew God. Of course, there are those who point out his character flaws and sins, along with those of other early leaders, in an effort to build a case that they weren't really Christians. That's like saying Abraham and David didn't have true relationships with God because they sinned. Although some historical sources point out that there were a few early American leaders who were Deists and humanistic in their views toward God, the words of George Washington and other founding fathers speak for themselves.

Note Washington's God-honoring statement at his inauguration on April 30, 1789, as the first president of the United States:

It would be peculiarly improper to omit, in this first official act, my fervent supplication to that Almighty Being, who rules over the universe, who presides in the councils of nations, and whose providential aids can supply every human defect, that His benediction may consecrate to the liberties and happiness of the people of the United States. . . . No people can be bound to acknowledge and adore the invisible hand which conducts the affairs of men more than the people of the United States. Every step by which they have advanced to the character of an independent nation seems to have been distinguished by some token of providential agency. . . . We ought to be no less persuaded that the propitious smiles of heaven can never be expected on a nation that disregards the eternal rules of order and right, which heaven itself has ordained.[5]

The above examples reflect only a few of the many times when our forefathers honored and called upon God for help. What was God's response? Did He answer? Was He involved in the history of America? The following story sheds light on the effectiveness of Washington's prayer life and God's involvement in the founding of this nation.

Entering the Virginia militia as a young officer, Washington had distinguished himself in combat during the French and Indian Wars, including the Battle of the Monongahela on July 9, 1755.

Fifteen years later an Indian chief spoke to Washington regarding that day.

I am a chief and ruler over my tribes and my influence extends far. I have traveled a long and weary path, that I might see the young warrior of the great battle. When I first beheld this chief, I called to my young men and said, "Mark yon tall and daring warrior? He is not of the red-coat tribe—he hath an Indian's wisdom, and his warriors fight as we do—himself alone is exposed. Quick, let your aim be certain, and he dies." Our rifles were leveled, but 'twas all in vain; a power mightier far than we shielded him from harm. He cannot die in battle. I am old, and soon shall be gathered to the great council fire of my fathers in the land of shades, but ere I go, there is something that bids me speak in the voice of prophecy: Listen! The Great Spirit protects that man, and guides his destinies—he will become the chief of nations, and a people yet unborn will hail him as the founder of a mighty empire.

Confirmation of this episode can be found in other historical records. At that battle, the 23-year-old colonel had two horses shot out from under him and four musket balls pass through his coat. There was nothing wrong with the Indians' marksmanship!

"Death," wrote Washington to his brother, Jack, "was leveling my companions on every side of me, but by the all-powerful dispensations of Providence, I have been protected."

This conviction was further shared by Samuel Davies, the famous Virginia clergyman, who wrote, "To the public I point out that heroic youth . . . whom I cannot but hope Providence has preserved in so signal a manner for some important service to his cou

    This was God's man, chosen for the
America's greatest crisis.[6]


Is there not a history? Indeed there is—a history
dence on God and of His faithfulness toward this
Hundreds more such examples could be cited. Apart fi
sovereign help, England would have crushed these floun
revolutionaries. Our forefathers were not perfect, but the
ruling role of God in their lives cannot be denied. Bringing
into the moment, John Adams said that the day on which
Declaration of Independence was signed

> will be the most memorable . . . in the history of America.
> I am apt to believe that it will be celebrated by succeed-
> ing generations, as the great anniversary festival. It
> ought to be commemorated, as the Day of Deliverance,
> by solemn acts of devotion to God Almighty. It ought to
> be solemnized with pomp and parade, with shows,
> games, sports, guns, bells, bonfires and illuminations,
> from one end of this continent to the other, from this
> time forward forevermore.
>     You will think me transported with enthusiasm, but
> I am not. I am well aware of the toil and blood and trea-
> sure that it will cost to maintain this Declaration, and
> support and defend these States. Yet through all the
> gloom I can see the rays of ravishing light and glory. I
> can see that the end is worth more than all the means.[7]

John Trumble, governor of Connecticut, said:

> Be roused and alarmed to stand forth in our just and
> glorious cause. Join . . . march on; this shall be your war-

for God, and for the cities of our God!

rar Hosts, the God of the armies of Israel,

M

nor wrote to the Board of Trade in England

ask an American, who is his master? He will tell

, nor any governor but Jesus Christ." This may

to the cry that was soon passed up and down the

rica by the Committees of Correspondence: *"No*

*sus!"* There was obviously no confusion or misun-

concerning the God or Savior they relied on. And I

uch separation of church and state (a phrase found

our Constitution) in these words.

less other examples could be given. As we fight for our

rpose in America, not only is there a history from which

but there is also a history to be written. And we hold the

forces bent on altering the God-intended future of this

on want to transform us from a Christian nation to a secu-

r one, but we do not have to allow this to happen. And though

we may not like to hear it, God will hold *us*, His people, account-

able for the history that is written. "If *my* people" (2 Chron. 7:14,

*NIV,* emphasis added) is still the condition for healing and God's

blessing.

## OUR DESTINY IS IN JEOPARDY

Our destiny was and is to be an example of what God will do for a nation "whose God is the LORD" (Ps. 33:12). *Please hear me, Body of Christ in America: that destiny is in jeopardy.* We were meant to partner with Him on Earth, just as Israel did, becoming a light to the other nations of the earth and sending the gospel of Jesus Christ from these shores to the ends of the earth. Though still happening to some degree, that history is now being altered. As stated earlier, we are now the leading exporter of pornography, as well as other forms of depravity through film and music. We are missionaries of filth! Some of the shocking history we're writing today will one day shame us. I wish it would now.

Though founded as a Christian nation, few Americans are now born-again Christians. As a nation we no longer adhere to the principles of Scripture, though our very form of government was patterned on Isaiah 33:22: "For the LORD is our judge [Judicial Branch], the LORD is our lawgiver [Legislative Branch], the LORD is our king [Executive Branch]; He will save us." Are we still a Christian nation? By faith only—that is, in word, not in deed.

Biblical standards of morality are no longer accepted. We actually allow homosexual "marriages" and "families." We pass out condoms to high school students, after teaching them about sex. Purity is mocked; immorality is lauded. The result? More than 40 percent of teenage girls get pregnant before reaching the age of 20. That's double the rate in England and 10 times that in the Netherlands. Sixty-six percent of students report having sex before leaving high school, and 25 percent of those sexually active teenagers contract a sexually transmitted disease.[9]

Many scientists, no longer hesitant to teach theory as fact, tell us we're made in the image of monkeys rather than God and are against even the sharing of biblical perspectives. No wonder life is cheap in America and we experiment on aborted babies, nonchalantly referring to them as "fetal tissue." Taking babies from the womb to the dumpster is now a deplorably shocking part of American history.

The madness must stop! We're writing a nauseating history, one over which our children and grandchildren will weep. If things don't change, the titles for our chapters of history will read:

- The Loss of a Godly Heritage in America
- America: The Forgotten Dream
- Once Great America, Destroyed from Within
- God Gave Her Time to Repent, But . . .

These are not ridiculous and far-fetched exaggerations. These alarming possibilities are even now in progress; some are nearly accomplished.

I want to change them!

I want to be a history maker!

I refuse to give this nation to the humanists, atheists and liberal politicians—those morally bankrupt individuals who want God and the Bible out of America. Though much ground has been lost to them, it is not too late. This is not their land, it is God's and ours! "The earth is the LORD's, and the fulness thereof" (Ps. 24:1, *KJV*).

Don't get me wrong. I'm not condoning blowing up abortion clinics, hanging witches or beating up homosexuals. God loves the sinner and so must we. But loving them doesn't mean giving them what they want, no more than it does with a spoiled child. Tolerance does not mean acceptance—and certainly not abdication.

The giants of sin and godlessness in our nation can be conquered and beheaded. The hearts of people can be won. We can alter the course of history but only if we recognize things for what they are. We must determine, like David, that we have had enough of the taunting giants coming against us in the name of their gods.

I plead with you, Church in America, it's time to daily and fervently claim promises such as, "Where sin abounded, grace did much more abound" (Rom. 5:20, *KJV*). Second Chronicles 7:14 (*KJV*) is still true: "If my people, which are called by my name, shall humble themselves, and pray, and seek my face, and turn from their wicked ways; then will I hear from heaven, and will forgive their sin, and will heal their land." I believe this with all my heart, and I live for this hope.

In thinking about hope-filled promises, I want to share one final encouraging thought about David's question, "Is there not a cause?" Interestingly, the word *zod* translated "cause," could be translated not only as "history" but also as "promise." "Is there not a promise?" David may have been demanding of Israel, *Don't we have some promises from God that we can stand on at this critical time? What about Deuteronomy 28:7:* "The LORD will cause your enemies who rise up against you to be defeated before you; they shall come out against you one way and shall flee before you seven ways." *And Joshua 1:3,5 declares:* "Every place on which the sole of your foot treads, I have given it to you just as I spoke to Moses. No man will be able to stand before you all the days of your life. Just as I have been with Moses, I will be with you; I will not fail you or forsake you."

> I refuse to give this nation to the humanists, atheists and liberal politicians—those morally bankrupt individuals who want God and the Bible out of America.

"We have clear promises from God," David was likely stating. "Let's claim them and go after this uncircumcised Philistine."

That's what I am saying to the Church in America! We're not at the mercy of the godless giants in our land, as shocking and large as they are (unless, of course, like Israel facing Goliath, *we* cower at their arrogance). We have promises to claim and a history to build on. Let's do it!

We must call upon God and go on the offensive. If enough of us do this, confessing the sins of America and appealing to

God for mercy, He will answer our prayers and pour out His Spirit on our nation again. Now is the time. Like David, we must face the giants *in the name of the Lord*, knowing that history—and the promises of God—are on our side.

And, beloved, history is not only on our side, *it really is in our hands!*

### History Maker

Is it true today that when people pray,
cloudless skies will break, kings and queens will shake?
Yes, it's true, and I believe it.
I'm living for You.

Is it true today that when people pray,
we'll see dead men rise and the blind set free?
Yes, it's true and I believe it.
I'm living for You.

I'm gonna be a history maker in this land.
I'm gonna be a speaker of truth to all mankind.
I'm gonna stand.
I'm gonna run into Your arms again.

Yes, it's true today that when people stand
with the fire of God and the truth in hand,
We'll see miracles. We'll see angels sing.
We'll see broken hearts making history.
Yes, it's true. And we believe it.
We're living for You.[10]

## CHAPTER THREE

# CROSSING OVER

The question is not *if* we and history are being produced; history is always being made—always going somewhere—and so are we. Nor is the real question whether or not we are part of making history. We're all history makers in one way or another. The actual question involves a couple of different aspects: First, what history are we making? And, second, are we making it by default, watching from the sidelines, or are we actively involved in the history-making process?

America is at a historical crossroads. Decisions we make now will determine our history for years to come. There are pivotal points in a nation's history—*kairos*[1] points in time—when things are extremely critical and strategic. Decisions made at these times are much more far-reaching in scope than is otherwise the case. *Please hear me, Church of America: we are at one of those pivotal points.* We are an Esther generation born to shift history at such a time as this. We are Israel at the Jordan. Will we cross over and face the giants in the land, or will we die in the wilderness as a has-been nation that lost its bearings? Will we receive a holy visitation from Christ, or will we miss our visitation, as Jerusalem did, causing Jesus to weep and pronounce judgment (see Luke 19:41-44)?

Many decisions we make are relatively inconsequential in the long haul. It is important to know, however, that some choices really are do or die, sink or swim. Yet others, while life-determining decisions, are often not obvious as such. For many people, the crisis is not obvious. Because of our nation's prosperity and the fact that we are at peace, many do not realize the critical nature of where we are. It is much easier to recognize and face the challenge when the need is obvious and the decision is forced upon us. Hitler gave Europe no choice—fight or be conquered. At Pearl Harbor the Japanese gave the United States no choice—fight or be conquered. Goliath gave Israel no choice—fight or become slaves. America's current situation is not as obvious as these examples.

## BLIND TO THE CRISIS

Refusing to believe that we are at a crisis point, we think we have plenty of time; but this is not true. America will either choose *now* to cross into a new place with God, or this nation will enter another 30- to 40-year season of downward moral spiraling, resulting in a further loss of inner strength and character. Having just come through such a cycle of erosion, we cannot endure another. We must recognize our true need, respond with holy desperation and seize our God-given opportunity to cross over into the new.

Jesus said to Jerusalem, "You did not recognize the time of your visitation" (Luke 19:44). Unfortunately, the word "visitation" does not clearly communicate what Christ was saying. He was not simply talking about coming for a visit. The Greek word is *episkope*, from which we get the words "bishop," "overseer" and "superintendent." Jesus was saying, "I came to cover you, to be your shepherd and bishop again. I wanted to take you as a mother hen would take her chicks and wrap you under my wings, covering and protecting you. But you did not recognize that" (see Luke 13:34).

We in America are currently receiving the same offer. God is giving us an opportunity to return to Him and to the promise of His loving care. He wants to show us once more that righteousness (not money, power or pleasure) exalts a nation. Jesus is knocking at our door, saying, "Will you receive Me back into this nation as your shepherd and bishop, allowing Me to cover, protect and lead you? Will you once more become a nation *under God*?" I pray that we choose His covering, *for if we do not, we are choosing further spiritual death and destruction.*

The way that brings life isn't always the simplest decision. The way of complacency may be the easiest and seem the most natural, but it might also be the most deadly. The path of least resistance can be fatal.

For years, the opening of "The Wide World of Sports" television program illustrated "the agony of defeat" with a painful ending to an attempted ski jump. The skier appeared in good form as he headed down the jump, but then, for no apparent reason, he tumbled head over heels off the side of the jump, bouncing off the supporting structure.

What viewers didn't know was that he chose to fall rather than finish the jump. Why? As he explained later, the jump surface had become too fast, and midway down the ramp, he realized if he completed the jump, he would land on the level ground, beyond the safe sloping landing area, which could have been fatal.

As it was, the skier suffered no more than a headache from the tumble.[2]

At this time in America we need to leave the seemingly safe ski slope. Sometimes the boat just has to be rocked. History makers are boat rockers. They are not "que sera sera" people but rather people who *choose* to make a difference, even when that means taking the most difficult way. At times, choosing life, ironically enough, can even mean choosing death. That was the choice for Christ the Savior, Stephen the martyr, Martin Luther King the reformer and countless unsung heroes of change. Many have gone to war, choosing life for others while it meant their own deaths. Sometimes the difficult and costly way simply must be chosen.

Change is imperative for us in America, and its price will involve prayer, fasting, sacrifice, repentance, moral change and going against the tide of public opinion. But these hard choices, the costly way, are what will truly preserve and produce life. Will godly history makers arise, *choosing* to be those who rock the boat? As a nation, will we die in the wilderness like Moses' generation, or will we cross over into God's blessing as the Joshua generation did?

## THE "HEBREW" IN US

Abraham was a cause-minded, history-making, crossing-over guy. Several months ago, God began to grip me with a verse about him. Genesis 14:13 uses the phrase "Abram the Hebrew." At first it seemed insignificant, but then I began to wonder why he was called a Hebrew. Where did this designation, first mentioned in this verse, come from? Finally, I decided to study the word in an effort to understand the meaning and discern why Abraham was called "the Hebrew."

The word for "Hebrew" is *ibriy*,[3] which originates from the word *abar*, meaning "to cross over or into; to pass by or into."[4] Basically, it means moving from one place to another. Sometimes *abar* is a very generic word for simply passing or crossing from one place to another—and is, in fact, used this way hundreds of times in the Old Testament. Other times the passing into or crossing over is a very significant, meaningful and life-changing experience.

Interestingly enough, because *abar* is a transition word, it also means "to penetrate,"[5] as in penetrating territory or even the human heart. And not trying to be overly dramatic or graphic, it is indeed a word used to designate the physical relations between a husband and wife that results in pregnancy. Yes, the word does mean to impregnate.[6] An *abar* experience with God can be so significant that we find ourselves pregnant with a new nature, mission, calling or understanding.

> As a nation, will we die in the wilderness like Moses' generation, or will we cross over into God's blessing as the Joshua generation did?

Abraham was a Hebrew because he chose to cross over with God, moving from the old into the new. "By faith Abraham, when he was called, obeyed by going out to a place which he was to receive for an inheritance; and he went out, not knowing where he was going" (Heb. 11:8). Choosing to obey God, he went to a new land, not knowing where he was going until God said to stop, all because he was called of God to cross over into something new. That's why one definition of a Hebrew, given by *Strong's Concordance,* is actually "one from the other side."[7] What a testimony!

As I further studied this word *abar* and its meaning of "crossing over and into," as well as the numerous occasions where it is used, I found several important *characteristics* of those who cross over. I also saw clearly the *results* of crossing over with the Lord. These characteristics and potential blessings are very pertinent to us as a nation today. As I stated earlier, America is at a crossroads. We are determining whether to be Abrahamic Hebrews at heart, crossing over into a new place, or whether to move further into complacent sterility and destruction.

Let's look at these Hebrew characteristics.

## Each Generation Has a Crossing Over Before Them

First, *each generation must have its own crossing over.* Every generation must choose to become a history-making Hebrew people. In Joshua 3:4, before crossing into their inheritance, the Israelites under Joshua were told to follow the Ark of the Covenant very carefully. "Do not come near it [in other words, stay far enough back, so everyone can see it], that you may know the way by which you shall go, for you have not passed [*abar*] this way before." God was saying to Joshua's generation, "I know you are descendants of Abraham, but you're not a Hebrew just because your grandfather was. You're a Hebrew when in your heart you choose to cross over. Every generation must have its own crossing. You haven't had *yours* yet." They chose to cross over into the new.

The previous generation that came out of Egypt had never become true Hebrews. They chose to make the wilderness their destiny and never crossed over. "Destiny Lost" became the final word on their history.

Judges 2:10 states that many years later Joshua's generation "also were gathered to their fathers; and there arose another generation after them who did not know the LORD, nor yet the work which He had done for Israel." What a tragedy—another non-crossing-over generation of Israelites! Joshua's generation had failed to instill a crossing-over spirit in them. As descendants of Abraham, they were Hebrews by blood but not in heart.

Sadly, history tells us there has never been a revival that has been carried on by the next generation. (The verdict is still out on the current revival taking place in Argentina.) This is because we haven't understood that each generation must have its own crossing over. God is asking our generation, the Church of America today, if we will become Hebrews and cross over into the new. Will we pay the price? Will we make the right choices? Will we rise up and become history makers, turning this nation back to God?

Never mind that our forefathers—the Washingtons, Adamses, Henrys, Lincolns and others—crossed over. Never mind the D. L. Moodys, Finneys, Cartwrights, Jonathan Edwardses and Billy Grahams who all crossed over. It's our turn. What will *we* do? The words of F. D. Roosevelt are very appropriate for us today: "This generation of Americans has a rendezvous with destiny!"

We have some important choices to make. We must righteously stand against sin, choosing to repent, fast and pray. We must choose unselfishness—giving of our time, energy and money. We need to make a difference in our communities—reaching out to the hurting, the homeless and those caught in poverty. It is time to increase our commitment to church and to those who are trying to make a difference. We need to support and help those who are working to bring about godly changes in our schools, government and nation. There is a cause and we must embrace it.

## God Crosses Over Ahead of Us

The second important truth concerning *abar*—crossing over—is that *God crosses ahead of us*. Joshua 3:11 tells us, "Behold, the ark of the covenant of the LORD of all the earth is crossing over ahead of you into the Jordan." Actually, a more literal translation would be, "Behold the Ark of the Covenant. The Lord of all the earth is crossing over ahead of you into the Jordan." God had always told Moses He would go before Israel into the land "as a consuming fire" (Deut. 9:3), destroying, subduing and driving out their enemies. He passed through (*abar*) Egypt on the night of Passover, striking the firstborn in the land while bringing deliverance to Israel (see Exod. 12:12).

When we're willing to cross into our inheritance, face the giants and possess our land, God promises always to cross ahead of us, preparing the way. So, not surprisingly, when Joshua found himself at Jericho, contemplating how to take that first city, he found the Lord already there. The Captain was waiting! Joshua didn't have to develop a strategy or battle plans; the Captain had already done it. It was as though the Lord was saying to him, "I promised I would cross ahead of you, Joshua, and prepare the way. I've been waiting for you. I already have the plan. Now here's how we're going to accomplish this victory."

When we choose to cross over, determining to repossess America, we'll find that our source of victory has gone before us. When we rise up in prayer for America, He will meet us. When we pray for our fallen schools, neighborhoods, government agencies and leaders, we'll find the Captain waiting with great strategy and empowerment. He will have already passed before us.

In the fall of 1998, while in prayer, the Lord showed me a picture of Himself on His white horse, as described in the book of Revelation. Dressed in full battle array, he and his mount were ready for war. The Lord had a lance in His hand and, as they stood on a huge map of the United States, He was listening for something. I knew He was waiting for instructions. Suddenly, when the directive was given, He spurred the horse and they took off, sprinting across America. Upon reaching His first destination, which, very significantly, was Washington, D.C., He stopped and struck the ground with His lance, and fire sprang forth.

They then waited for the next instructions. Very anxious to be on the move again, the Lord was poised for action as the horse impatiently stomped its hooves. Then, at the next directive, they would once again charge across America to the next location, He would strike the ground with the lance, and fire would burst forth. This same scenario occurred without pattern 8 to 10 times as the Lord crisscrossed the country.

I realized this was a very literal picture of the Lord Himself getting ready to cross this nation to bring His fire of cleansing and revival. I believe this has now begun—the Lord impressed on my heart at the beginning of this year that it had started. As so accurately portrayed by this picture, the Lord really does cross before us in this nation, igniting His fire, preparing the way for revival and change.

### Our Crossing Over Terrifies Our Enemies

Third, it is encouraging to know that becoming a Hebrew, or crossing over, *terrifies our enemies*. In Joshua 2:9-14, Rahab of Jericho told the spies how terrified the people were of them. Their "hearts melted and no courage remained in any man." They knew God was going to give Israel the land, and they had lived in terror of that for 40 years. Their fear is also evidenced in Joshua 5:1:

Now it came about when all the kings of the Amorites who were beyond the Jordan to the west, and all the kings of the Canaanites who were by the sea, heard how the LORD had dried up the waters of the Jordan before the sons of Israel until they had crossed, that their hearts melted, and there was no spirit in them any longer, because of the sons of Israel.

Satan knows that when we, God's people, make the right choices to obey God, to cross over—*to be history makers*—he cannot overpower us. He sometimes stops us with fear, as he did the generation that came out of Egypt and the Israelites through Goliath; and he sometimes defeats us through complacency, but he can never stop us by overpowering us. He has not defeated us in America by force. He has accomplished it through deceit, sin, moral depravity, turning away from God and a complacent Church.

Satan's most effective assault has been in bringing about a shift in our perspective on truth. Most Americans have chosen to reject absolute moral truth in favor of relativism. Not a change that happened overnight, this "new thinking" has infiltrated our belief system during the past several decades, resulting in the notion that a person is the center of his or her universe and is, therefore, responsible for determining what is right and wrong, appropriate and inappropriate, useful and useless, significant and insignificant. This transformation has done more to undermine the health and stability of American society than anything else, opening the door to immorality, humanism, violence, lack of character and loss of core values such as honesty, decency and integrity.

We cannot simply blame the world—those who do not know Christ—for the condition of America. God has never predicated revival, deliverance or the healing of a nation on the action of unbelievers. In the Scriptures, He always puts the condition for restoration on us, His people. This brings responsibility, yes, but also hope—we are not at the mercy of the godless. If we, the people of God, do what He tells us to do, America will change. Our enemy knows this, so he intimidates us with the size of the task or lulls us to sleep through complacency and apathy—choices by default. We are at a crucial point where we must consciously *choose* to believe in the cause, cross over and go forward. Our enemy is terrified of that possibility, knowing that if we do cross over, he will be powerless to stop us.

## People Who Cross Over Are in Covenant

Fourth, Hebrews—those who cross over—*are people of covenant.* Genesis 15 tells of God entering into a covenant with Abraham and of the animal sacrifice being cut into pieces. Verse 17 says, "It came about when the sun had set, that it was very dark, and behold, there appeared a smoking oven and a flaming torch which passed between these pieces. On that day the LORD made a covenant with Abram."

The word *abar* is used for the torch—the fire of God—passing between the pieces of the sacrifice, which indicated God had received it as an acceptable covenantal offering. He, the Hebrew God, and Abraham, the Hebrew man, were now in covenant. "You crossed over to me, Abraham," God was saying. "Now, I'm crossing over to you." In covenant with God—what a declaration!

Much could be said about the significance of covenant; entire books have been written on the subject. I want to simply emphasize the partnering and sharing aspect. In a true covenant, resources, friends, enemies and spoils were all shared. If you were in covenant with a person, their enemies became yours, and you were *required* to fight for one another. Exemplifying this, Joshua fought for the Gibeonites in honor of a covenant, even though they had deceived Israel into making the covenant with them (see Joshua 9—10). God fought for His covenant partners, Abraham and Israel, and they prevailed. Likewise, we can possess the land because of our covenantal joining with the Lord.

Covenant partners also share assets. Because we are in covenant with God, that which He owns also belongs to us. Psalm 24:1 says, "The earth is the LORD's, and all it contains, the world, and those who dwell in it." Since the earth is His, it is our inheritance as well. And because enemies are shared, *our* enemies—Satan and his strongholds, not people—are really *God's* enemies. We will defeat Satan and free the people, because we are in covenant with the Lord.

Notice the powerful truth that when David the history maker faced Goliath, he never once called him by name. David always called him "the uncircumcised Philistine." Why? Because circumcision was a sign of the covenant. David was saying to all of Israel and to the giant, "I am in covenant with God; you are not. That means I win, you lose. It means you're not just my enemy, you are God's enemy. The battle is not mine, it's the Lord's, and He will give you into my hand" (see 1 Sam. 17:47).

If we obey God and do things His way, He will fight for us and give us the ability to take the land. We must look at the giants (not the people) in our nation and boldly proclaim, "You will lose because we are in covenant with God and you are not." Then we must take action!

## People Who Cross Over Are Identified by a Sign of Covenant

The fifth characteristic I found about crossing over follows right along with the previous one: *Hebrews are a circumcised people.* After Israel crossed over into Canaan, the first thing God required of them was circumcision (see Josh. 5:2-3). The cutting off of the male foreskin was a sign of covenant and separation to God. He was saying to them, "Now that you're Hebrews and in covenant with Me, you must be set apart unto Me." Our circumcision in the new covenant, of course, is of the heart whereby we join the Lord covenantally and become set apart unto Him.

Please hear this incredible truth: Not only were these Israelites circumcised—set apart relationally and covenantally unto the Lord—but so also was their inheritance, the land. Joshua 4:7 states that the waters of the Jordan were "cut off." This phrase was used twice in this verse to describe God's rolling back the Jordan River, allowing them to enter the land (see also Josh. 3:16). The word translated "cut off" is the Hebrew word for circumcision, the cutting off of the foreskin.[8] I believe God was saying, "Not only are *you* being set apart in covenant unto Me, but *the land* I'm giving you is also being set apart covenantally unto Me. Not only are *you* being circumcised, but I am also circumcising *the land*."

Another example in Joshua 3:5 confirms the land's being included in the blessing and covenant. God told Joshua to "consecrate," or make holy, the people, which is the word *qadash*. He then told Joshua in chapter 5 verse 15 that the land is "holy" (*qodesh*). Same word. Not only had the people been set apart unto God and become holy, but so also had the land. God crossed ahead of them, circumcising it and making it holy. Why should this surprise us? Since land can be defiled (see Num. 35:33), why can't it be holy? Didn't Deuteronomy 28:4 say He would bless the produce of the ground? Absolutely. When we come into covenant with the Lord, so should our possessions.

When the Pilgrims entered into covenant with God in this nation, He honored this. They dedicated the land to God and set it apart to Him. Not only were the people blessed, but so also was the entire nation. We must claim this covenantal blessing and by faith call our land holy and set apart unto God.

Notice also that Jesus, the Captain who met Joshua at Jericho, did not wait until all of the idols and giants were gone from the land or until after Jericho had been taken to call the land holy. He said it before these things took place. How could this be? Because they had entered into covenant with Him and circumcised themselves, He was able to also bless their inheritance. We in America don't have to wait until we have conquered all the idolatry and sin before we can say this land is holy and belongs to God. It has already been set apart unto Him and is holy. We can decree it by faith now.

## People Who Cross Over Require Great Faith

Becoming a Hebrew—crossing over—*requires great faith*. Joshua 1:2 states, "Moses My servant is dead; now therefore arise, cross *this* Jordan" (emphasis added). Not the Jordan River of six months ago or six months from now, but *this* Jordan. Why is it so significant that Israel was to cross this Jordan? Because this Jordan was in flood stage (see Josh. 3:15). Instead of crossing a waist-deep, 30- to 40-foot wide stream that they could have carried children and possessions across, they were going to have to cross a raging, flooded river that was probably as much as a mile wide. *It was going to require a lot of faith to begin this crossing.* And the waters didn't begin to roll back until the feet of the priests carrying the Ark of the Covenant touched the water!

Joshua 3:16 states that the people crossed over the Jordan "opposite Jericho." Of all the places where God could have allowed Israel to cross, He chose perhaps the most formidable city of all. It was as if He said, "I want you to cross here. I don't want you to try and start with the smallest and the easiest. I want you to cross *this* Jordan, *right here at Jericho*."

God was, in essence, saying to Israel, "We're going to get something established right up front. Making history with Me—taking this land—is going to require faith. But once you push through the difficulty of believing and see My mighty hand at work, it will be established in your heart once and for all that you can trust Me. From then on we can do anything."

In my calling with the Lord, so often when He gives me a new place to cross into—a new assignment, responsibility, challenge—it begins with great steps of faith.

When God began to speak to me in January of 1999 about going into various parts of the nation, my preference would have been to start with some "easy" places. I knew He was giving me a new assignment of going to specific cities to work toward revival—calling for intercession, repentance and breakthrough. I figured I would begin with some small towns, but the Lord spoke to my heart that the first place was to be Washington, D.C. He was not going to let me start with the possibility of judging things from a natural perspective. God wouldn't allow me to move into a place of unbelief. Since that time over two years ago, I have probably made 12 to 15 prayer and ministry journeys into the D.C. area.

Every one of us will have a different assignment. Your calling may never be to go beyond your own city. You may never need to travel as I do. But whatever assignments the Lord gives you, you will need to rise up in faith, accept them and take the necessary steps to fulfill them.

## People Who Cross Over Make Preparation

The seventh principle of crossing over sounds so simple and basic, but believe me, it isn't. Becoming a Hebrew—crossing over, taking on giants, changing nations—*requires preparation.* Joshua 1:11 states, "Prepare provisions for yourselves, for within three days you are to cross this Jordan, to go in to possess the land which the LORD your God is giving you." God said to Israel, and He is also saying to us, that making history means planning. We must prepare. In order to change this nation, we must make preparations by altering how we think, the way we live and where we spend our time and money. We will need to care more, pray more, serve more and give more. When a nation goes to war, it makes preparations for war. And when we decide to war for a nation, we must realize right up front that it will cost us.

When God called me to the nation in 1999, everything in my life changed. My schedule was already as full as I wanted it to be, but it became even busier. My ministry changed as God readjusted my focus. My prayer times, study times, family times, traveling schedule, pastoral responsibilities, recreation and spare times—all of them were affected and changed. I wrote more books and my ministry expanded and became busier, which brought changes to my office staff. The challenges grew much more demanding, and as this happened I had to readjust my ways of thinking.

Again, the changes and challenges you experience will be different from mine. Most of you will probably not be called to travel and minister to a nation as I do, but there will still be adjustments pertinent to your way of life and the particular calling God has given you. Everything changes when God gives an assignment.

God is giving us an opportunity in this nation to cross over with Him, to write the history He desires for America. Let's become cause-minded people, history makers, Hebrews at heart!

## CHAPTER FOUR

# THE FRUITS OF CROSSING OVER

God is giving us an opportunity to see true change in America, to cross over into a fresh time of renewal and revival, to preserve our destiny. When we cross over with faith and in preparation—in the wisdom God provides—we need to recognize that He is with us and that our enemies will be frightened by godly courage. Even more, when we cross over our personal Jordans—to be Hebrews—there are fruits that are born from our act of faith and His presence in our lives. Here are seven fruits that I have identified.

# CROSSING OVER

## The Fruit of Jubilee

First, becoming a Hebrew—crossing over—*releases the fruit of Jubilee*! If you understand Jubilee, that should excite you! The blowing of the Jubilee trumpet marked the beginning of Israel's 50-year Jubilee celebration. At Jubilee, slaves were freed, property was restored to its original owner, and debts were forgiven (see Lev. 25:8-17). It was a glorious fresh start for everyone. The word used to describe the blowing of the Jubilee trumpet is *abar*, used because of the wind "passing through" the trumpet. It no doubt represented the wind or breath of God, which brings life, freedom and new beginnings—the fruit of Jubilee. Psalm 89:15 says, "How blessed are the people who know the joyful sound [blast of the trumpet]!"[1]

The Israelites blew these Jubilee trumpets at Jericho (see Josh. 6:8) and then shouted, and the walls fell down. God huffed and puffed . . . well, maybe not. But the God of Jubilee blew His mighty breath, and the walls of opposition fell. That is Jubilee—city taking and history making.

God desires to release His holy breath of deliverance to this nation once more, giving us Jubilee. He desires the trumpet sound of freedom to resonate again as His wind blows across America. Deliverance! Slavery broken off of people's hearts! These things are possible *now*. We must clearly sound the blast of Jubilee, declaring that the Lord our deliverer is crossing into our nation again. Let's cross with Him, history makers.

## Spirit-Filled Life

Second, the crossing over results in a *Spirit-filled life*. It was very fascinating to me that the word *abar* was used in Ezekiel 47 to describe the experience of crossing into each level of the river.

This river, representing the Holy Spirit, flowed out of the Temple and started as a trickle, then reached the ankles, the knees, the waist and finally became a river one had to swim in. *At every level of the river, Ezekiel had to pass, or cross into, it.*

We must move, or cross into, the various levels of the river of God's Spirit, drinking freely of each. God wants to fill us with the Spirit at each level of its flow and in every part of our lives. We are filled to one level, then the next and the next. Hebrews stay filled with the Spirit. This, and only this, can make us history makers. It is not by human might or power but by the Holy Spirit that we will prevail (see Zech. 4:6). Revival is born of the Spirit, strategies are released by the Spirit, unity must be of the Spirit, conversions are brought about by the Spirit—we must cross into every level of the Spirit!

I believe God wants and is waiting to release a fresh impartation of Holy Spirit life into the churches of America. From there it will flow out of the sanctuary, just like the river in Ezekiel, and into the dry places of the land: streets, homes, offices, schools, parks, wherever there are hungry people. And as it says of this river in Ezekiel, everything it touches will live (see Ezek. 47:9)!

Please hear my heart, Church of America. If we do not see a mighty deluge of revival, there is no hope for this nation. Small, incremental seasons of fruitfulness will not bring sufficient change. We are simply too far down the road of spiritual death; we are in trouble. A mighty revival, a thunderous outpouring of Holy Spirit power that rocks America to her knees is necessary. Please cry out for it with me, fervently and often.

## Pregnant with God's Glory

Third, Hebrews become *pregnant with God's glory*. What a statement! What a hope! You will recall that two of the definitions of *abar* are to penetrate and impregnate. When in obedience we cross over with God, He can then penetrate our hearts, planting His seeds of life and truth in us. As He penetrates us with these seeds, we become pregnant with His life and glory.

In Exodus 33:19 and 34:6, God "passed by" (*abar*) Moses on the mountain. More than a simple passing by, however, it was a passing *to*, followed by a speaking to, and then God passed by Moses with His glory. When he left that experience, Moses was so pregnant with the glory of God that his face shone! Though we may not glow, when we cross over with God and He comes to us, He fills us with His Spirit and we, too, become pregnant with His glory.

The two biblical concepts of glory have to do with *weightiness,* seen in the Hebrew word *kabowd,* and *recognition,* seen in the Greek word *doxa.* When the glory of God is released, it brings His heavy weight of authority (*kabowd*) to save and deliver. His glory will settle over our land with a heavy hand, breaking the powers of darkness over our nation. God will then be *recognized* (*doxa*) again in our land.

This must begin in us, the Body of Christ. God must first be recognized in and through us, just as He needed to be in Israel. He works through His people, not independently of them. If we will accept the challenge, choosing to be history makers, God's glory will come to us. We will then have the strength and weight to possess the land.

**Resurrection Power**

The fourth principle of crossing over is another important result—becoming a Hebrew *brings resurrection power to us.* When we are filled with God's Spirit, His glory comes and we are then filled with the resurrection life of God. Joshua 1:11 states, "Within three days you are to cross this Jordan." In the Bible, "three days" often refers prophetically to resurrection. When the Israelites crossed the Jordan River and the Ark of the Covenant went in first, without doubt it foreshadowed what happened centuries later when Christ went into death (Jordan River) and came out on the other side (Canaan) with resurrection life. The Israelites' crossing with the Ark is a prophetic picture of our being crucified with Christ (see Gal. 2:20) and then coming forth in resurrection. I do not want to take the time to theologically demonstrate all of this, but no true biblical scholar would disagree with this symbolism.

My point is simply that crossing over brings God's resurrection power to us. We then begin to fulfill verses such as Acts 4:33 (*KJV*): "And with great power gave the apostles witness of the resurrection of the Lord Jesus: and great grace was upon them all." "Great" is from the Greek adjective *megas*, from which we get the English prefix "mega." Mega grace brought mega power and mega revival. The entire message of the Early Church in the book of Acts, and the entire reason for their success, was the power of the resurrection of Christ. And the power of Christ's resurrection is all about the miraculous. God wants to give witness to the world that Jesus is still alive.

> **If we make the right decisions in this nation at this time, we will see a great return of the miraculous. . . . on the streets and in our schools, homes and offices.**

Please hear me. If we make the right decisions in this nation at this time, we will see a great return of the miraculous. God will work miracles on the streets and in our schools, homes and offices. He will set people free and deliver them. His power will come and overwhelm the enemy, and we will move into an extraordinary season of resurrection life. This season will manifest not only in the lives of the lost but also in our personal lives—delivering, freeing and transforming us in every area. This wonderful outpouring occurs for those who cross over with God—and it can be a reality for this entire nation.

## Power of Multiplication

Fifth, crossing over brings *the power of multiplication*. In 1 Kings 19, Elijah, after his battle with the prophets of Baal and his stand against Ahab and Jezebel, somehow found himself discouraged and overcome by the *spirit* of Jezebel (not the woman). He was isolated, depressed, weary, afraid; and he had become so discouraged that he wanted to die (see 1 Kings 19:4). God's solution was to send him to Horeb, "the mountain of God" (1 Kings 19:8).

There, Elijah found himself in a cave. A cave is a dark place, similar to the present condition of America, but God can be found there. Many scholars believe this was the same cave, or cleft, that Moses was in when God passed to and by him (see Exod. 33:19-23). And the same things occurred with Elijah as with Moses. The Lord was *abar*, passing by (see 1 Kings 19:11). In the same way that He made Moses pregnant with His glory, He made Elijah pregnant with a word. God instructed Elijah to do three things: anoint Elisha as a successor and anoint Jehu and Hazael as kings.

Think about it. At the time when Elijah felt the weakest, God came to him and spoke a word—and Elijah found himself pregnant with the power of multiplication. He was able to give a double portion of the anointing in him to Elisha. And Jehu, after being anointed by him, finished the job of overthrowing evil Ahab and Jezebel, a job that Elijah could only begin. Out of his weakness flowed strength.

God can do this for us as well. When we cross over with God and He crosses over to us, it will bring us the power of multiplication. What will that mean? Salvations! And the raising up of another generation of Christians in America who will go far beyond us in taking the gospel of Christ to the world and seeing people set free. Perhaps it will mean a generational transfer of giftings and anointings, resulting in salvations by the thousands, hundreds of thousands and millions.

The power of multiplication comes through the Hebrew anointing and can begin to manifest even when, like Elijah, we are at our lowest point. What a gracious God!

### Broken People Gain the Inheritance of Being God's People

The sixth result is that those who choose to be Hebrews become *broken, transformed people and eventually the Israel of God*. Three times in his life, as recorded in Genesis 31—32, Jacob crossed rivers. These crossings were more than just casual crossings. They were very significant and hold great symbolism for us.

Genesis 31:21 records the first crossing. On his way back to face Esau, Jacob first had to cross the Euphrates, the river whose name means "break forth." Consistent with the symbolism, God was beginning a process of breaking Jacob's conniving, thieving and swindling nature. When we cross over with God, He is committed to our transformation.

This is true both individually and corporately. God is committed to the transformation of this nation. To do so, He has been bringing America, especially the Church in America, through a process of breaking. He has convicted us, exposed our proud hearts, graciously allowed many of our self-initiated efforts to fail and brought us to much repentance. Many have responded by allowing the Holy Spirit to go deep within, rooting out flesh desires and weaknesses. I pray that we, like Jacob, keep crossing.

In Genesis 32:22, on the same journey back to face his sin and deception, Jacob crossed the Jabbok, the river whose name means "pouring out." God began Jacob's breaking process at the Euphrates, and at Jabbok he was poured out. There Jacob wrestled with the angel of the Lord all night. What was God's purpose for this wrestling? He wanted to once and for all pour from Jacob the Jacob nature. To do so, God first removed his possessions from him. They had all been sent ahead of him, and now Esau, no doubt, controlled them. Moments before Jacob had been wealthy; but now, as far as he knew, he had nothing.

His family had also been sent on ahead and there was the very real possibility of losing them as well. Hoping, I'm sure, that they would be spared if Esau killed him, Jacob surely realized they could become slaves, as well as widows and orphans. And if that wasn't enough, God began to get even more personal in this emptying process. He touched the socket of Jacob's thigh and dislocated it, and for the rest of his life Jacob would walk with a limp. In Scripture, the thigh is often symbolic of personal strength.

God was showing Jacob, "No longer are you going to believe you can accomplish things independently of me. I am going to break the Jacob mind-set in you that thinks you can connive and scheme your way through everything. I'm going to make you dependent on Me, taking everything, including your own strength. For the rest of your life, you will walk with a blessed limp to remind you of your need for Me."

Finally, He poured from Jacob his name, which speaks of identity and nature. "What is your name?" asked the angel. "And [in shock of realization, whispering] he said, Jacob [supplanter, schemer, trickster, swindler]!" (Gen. 32:27, *AMP*). God went to the very core of his identity—who Jacob really was—and began to pour it out of him. Finally, when the pouring out had been completed, God declared, "No longer are you Jacob. You are now My Israel. Emptied of self, now you can be My prince, one who overcomes and prevails by the Spirit, not the flesh. I can not only do *for* you, but now I can also do *through* you" (Sheets's paraphrase).

What an amazing picture of what God currently wants to accomplish in the Church of America! He is asking, "Will you give up being Jacob and become My Israel? Will you become My people, My voice, choosing to be history makers with Me? You've been selfish long enough. Will you allow Me to pour all self out of you so that I can bless you and make you a blessing to the world and to this nation as well?"

## Meeting God Face-to-Face

Jacob's third crossing, this time over the Jordan, reveals the seventh fruit of being a Hebrew—and what a wonderful one it is! After the breaking (Euphrates) and the pouring (Jabbok), Jacob crossed Penuel, which means "the face of God." Hebrews are those who *meet God face-to-face*. The emptying of self brings purity, which Jesus said will result in seeing God (see Matt. 5:8).

Not only will we see *Him* more clearly, but He will also open our eyes to *see as He sees*. We will begin to see the nation as He sees it, understanding our true condition. We'll see the hurting as He sees them, weeping with Him over their pain and loneliness. We will no longer live for self but for Him and others. This is the result of crossing Penuel and seeing Him face-to-face. Once it occurs, like Jacob, we will never be the same.

In John 9, Jesus passed by a blind man. Though a Greek word for "passing" is used, it is the same concept as that of the Hebrew word—passing by, or passing to, someone. Jesus was questioned about whether this man was blind because of his sin or his parents' sin, a common question in that day. He responded that this wasn't the issue; rather, it was that God wanted to manifest His glory through the man.

Then Jesus did something very interesting and amazing. He spit on the ground, made clay by mixing the dirt and spit and rubbed it on the man's eyes. Of course, we know that in Christ's spit was the DNA of God. In a very literal sense, God took of His DNA, mixed it with the dust of the earth—just as He did in Genesis—and brought forth a miracle. His DNA on the man's eyes overcame the blindness and they were opened. The first thing this man saw was Jesus, and his life was transformed forever. He was no longer a beggar but an evangelist. What a testimony![2]

God wants to open our eyes in this nation. If we cross to Him, He will come to us and bring healing. Then we can once again become God's colaborers in the earth.

Interestingly, until Jacob's experience at Penuel, you will never find him calling God *his* God. And you will never find others speaking to Jacob and referring to God as his God. In Genesis 31:5; 31:42 and 32:9, he calls Him "the God of my father." The Lord Himself spoke to Jacob in Genesis 26:24 and 28:13 saying, I am "the God of your father." Even Laban, his father-in-law, said in Genesis 31:29, "The God of your father."

But after these crossings—the breaking, the pouring out and his seeing the face of God—Jacob built an altar and called it El-Elohe-Israel, which means "God, the God of Israel" (see Gen. 33:20). When he named this altar, the Israel he was referring to was not a race of people, nor was it a land. He was talking about himself, he who had just had his name changed from Jacob to Israel. When he wrote "God, the God of Israel" on the altar, he was saying, "He is not just the God of my father, not just the God of my grandfather. He is *my* God. I'm a Hebrew!"

When we cross over with Him, He becomes our God. Our heavenly Father is waiting for the Church of America to experience our own crossing over by which He becomes not only the God of our forefathers, not only the God who is mentioned on money or in the text of our Constitution, but a God who is *our* God—today. A God we know intimately and partner with personally.

## Building Memorials

There is one final and beautiful picture of becoming a Hebrew— the eighth fruit from crossing over—that I want to share with you. Hebrews *build memorials*. After Joshua and the Israelites crossed into the land, God told them to build two memorials: one in the Jordan riverbed and one on the Canaan, or inheritance, side of the Jordan. These memorials were to signify God's faithfulness and Israel's crossing over into the new as history makers. The previous generation wouldn't cross, but they did. They were going to take their inheritance and possess their land.

Notice that they were not told to build a memorial on the wilderness side of defeat, unbelief, wandering and purposelessness. The point is clear: God was telling them, "I don't want you to remember the failures; don't build memorials to them. I don't want you to walk in condemnation, grieving over your past mistakes." Yes, we must repent for our sins and turn from wickedness; but when God cleanses us, He wants us to move on, not wallow in the shame of who we've been. His desire is for us to move into who and what we can be.

I believe He is saying to America now, "If you allow Me, I will heal you, deliver you and help you write a new history. Memorials will not be built to your shame. We'll build them on the overcoming side of the crossing."

America, let's cross over with Him.

## CHAPTER FIVE

# Is There Not a Strategy?

I realize that the picture I have painted of America's current condition is bleak. And, unfortunately, I believe it is an accurate picture. However, as stated earlier in the book, I do have hope for America. The God who founded this nation is great and gracious. His deep, passionate love for this nation will not be denied. Because He is saying, "It is not too late for America," I still have hope for her.

## God's Passion for America

God shared His passion for America with me in October of 2000 when He somehow powerfully touched my heart with His. On a Wednesday night, for three-and-a-half hours, He allowed me to help Him cry over our nation. As I felt God's aching heart for

America, there was such an overwhelming intensity that I thought my own heart would break in two. I didn't know it was possible to weep from so deep within—not from my head or from my emotions but from deep in my heart.

A few days later, through the continued intensity of this burden, the Lord led me to issue a prayer alert for the upcoming presidential election. This alert ultimately went to millions of people, resulting in a great mobilization of prayer for God's person to be placed in office. The crucial nature of this prayer alert became extremely obvious as the election was held. And then, even when the election was finished, the identity of the next president had not yet been determined. The high level of spiritual warfare was very apparent. There were many times in the ensuing weeks when the situation looked very bleak. But there was a cause—our nation desperately needed a president through whom God could work.

At that pivotal point in our nation's history, God's people made a choice to cross over. As a result, God gave us a sincere, humble man who loves God and through whom He can work to accomplish His purposes.

I realize there are sincere believers who disagree with me. I know that minorities, especially in America, feel their cause is much safer in the hands of Democrats. I respect these positions and understand the passion with which they are held. However, I simply believe it was absolutely imperative that God have someone as our president who was very open to Him and walked in righteousness. To me, the entire ordeal was never about Republican or Democrat issues.

My wife and I, and a few others from our church in Colorado Springs, attended the inauguration of President George W. Bush. It was worth every minute of standing in the extremely cold rain, as well as the many previous hours of prayer and fasting, when I watched and heard him end his swearing-in by saying with great conviction, "So help me, God." Upon the uttering of those words, one well-known minister in attendance was heard to say, "The curse is broken off of America." I, too, believe that it marked a new beginning. We are, indeed, seeing God's grace upon us to heal and save our nation. However, many—including myself—do not believe this would have happened without the massive prayer effort that took place.

Just as God gave a strategy of prayer that shaped the election, He also wants to give us other strategies for turning America back to Him. Pertinent to this is another meaning of the word "cause" in 1 Samuel 17:29 (*KJV*). It is the Old Testament word for the "word" of the Lord. When David asked, "Is there not a cause?" the question could have been translated, "Is there not a word [from the Lord]?"

Whereas the concept of a promise involves something in the past to which we can stake our faith, a word from the Lord is a directive for today. David may also have been asking, "Isn't there a strategy that someone has heard from God about how to deal with this giant?"

## GOD'S STRATEGIC PLANS FOR REVIVAL

Strategies from the Lord can come in various dimensions and scope. They may be anything from prayer-walking a neighborhood to prayer-blanketing the nation. The ministry of Focus on the Family is one of God's strategies for bringing healing and wholeness to the families in America. God brought forth Promise Keepers as a strategy to powerfully impact men toward godliness. The Call, a gathering of 400,000 young people on The Mall in Washington, D.C. in September 2000, to fast and pray for America, was a strategy from God—a word of the Lord—for breakthrough. Starting a prayer meeting in your home could be a strategy that impacts your neighborhood, or God may initiate an outreach program as a strategy to touch a city.

Without a doubt, God has strategies for us to implement to turn this nation around. These will be revealed through pastors, businessmen, moms, students, grandparents, community leaders, office workers, teachers—anyone who is listening to hear a word from the Lord. We must believe that God has a strategy for America. When these plans are followed, they release an authority from the Lord that opens doors of breakthrough, revival and healing.

Shortly after I spearheaded prayer for the presidential election, God began a remarkable series of confirmations in my life regarding the authority that He wants to strategically release in America. It had to do with prayer for the election but was not limited to that situation. This was the most amazing series of confirmations I have ever received, showing me that God was indeed speaking to me about our nation. Let it encourage you.

> Without a doubt, God has strategies for us to implement to turn this nation around. When these plans are followed, they release an authority from the Lord that opens doors of breakthrough.

- It began on a cross-country flight. I noticed that my departure time was 2:22, I was seated in row number 22 and the total travel time was 2 hours and 22 minutes. My first thought was, *What a strange coincidence!* Then the Lord reminded me that He had been speaking to me from Isaiah 22:22, "I will set the key of the house of David on his shoulder, when he opens no one will shut, when he shuts no one will open." *Would God do something like this to bring me confirmation?* I wondered.

· A couple of days later I received a phone call from a spiritual father in my life. While in prayer, he had felt the Lord prompt him to call me and give me Isaiah 22:22, emphasizing the phrase, *the key of David.* He said, "God is giving you a key of authority in this nation."

· I then went to Washington, D.C., on a ministry trip, and a trusted intercessor friend of mine gave me a gift at the meeting. She said the Lord had impressed her months earlier to buy it for me, with the instruction that He would let her know when to give it to me. It was a beautiful silver key, and her words to me were, "This is the key of the city."

· Another man, knowing nothing about this, came to me after that meeting with three keys and said, "This morning I felt impressed to bring you these three keys." He, too, realized they symbolized spiritual authority. Matthew 16:19 states, "I will give you the keys of the kingdom of heaven; and whatever you shall bind on earth shall have been bound in heaven, and whatever you loose on earth shall have been loosed in heaven."

· A week later I was in San Diego and a friend of mine, Chuck Pierce, said that God had led him to give me a key. He had been given this key in New York by people who said it represented a revival anointing for America. Chuck said, "The Lord impressed me to give it to you."

· After that service, another man gave me three more keys, saying he had been impressed by the Lord to do so. Incredibly, "222" was on each of these keys.

- A couple of weeks later, I was in California again to meet and pray with my friend Lou Engle. He said to me, "God has been speaking to me about Isaiah 22:22. I've even had dreams about the number 22 and this verse. And at a meeting I led recently, the number of my hotel room was 222."

- After I came home from that meeting and shared this with our church, a young man in our congregation said to me, "Just today God directed me to Isaiah 22:22. I felt it was a verse for the Church."

- Another lady at the service had been awakened from a dream at 2:22 a.m. and heard the Lord speak to her about those numbers.

- Still another lady at the service, a visiting pastor's wife from New England, had also had a dream the previous night. In her dream there was a man with an old set of keys. She asked him, "What are you doing with those?" He replied that he was going to throw them away, because they were just old keys. In the dream she said to the man, "Please don't throw them away. They are precious. Can I have them?" He then gave her the keys.

Over the course of those few weeks, I had no fewer than 25 supernatural confirmations that God was speaking to me about keys of authority and relating it to Isaiah 22:22. I have never had anything like this happen to me before.

According to Isaiah 22:22, the keys symbolized spiritual keys of authority to open doors that no man can close and to close doors that no man can open. God was clearly saying, "I am giving you authority—keys—to impact the nation." Though the occurrences were happening to me, I know the word was for the entire Body of Christ, not just for me. We really have been given keys of authority from God to shift this nation. We must use them, opening doors that can't be closed by Satan or any person and closing doors of evil and destruction. We do this by prayer and obedience.

You can probably tell that I love to study word pictures and symbolism from the Old Testament. God often speaks to me through this method of study, bringing me revelation. During the intense time of prayer regarding the presidential election, especially during the initial visitation time that October evening, the Lord deeply impressed in my heart the thought, *I am calling this nation to Shechem.* Since everything else I felt during that encounter with the Lord has proved to be very accurate, I have great confidence that this thought is accurate as well.

## Calling America Back to Shechem

What could God mean by saying He was calling America back to Shechem? Hidden in the passages of Scripture involving Shechem, are there keys to crossing over and making godly history? Yes. Here are a few of them.

Shechem is the place where God first spoke to Abraham about giving him the land of Canaan (see Gen. 12:7). Symbolically, Shechem has everything to do with *inheritance* and is indeed *the place of promise.* If God is calling America back to Shechem, He is saying, "I want you to reclaim your inheritance. I gave you this land and partnered with you in the establishment of it. This is your inheritance, Body of Christ." Though parts of the land are owned by those who do not know the Lord, in reality this nation belongs to God. The land, the wealth, even the animals and people—all belong to God. He wants us—those who walk with Him—to lay hold of the inheritance He gave us when our nation was founded.

Second, as clearly shown in Genesis 12:2-3, Shechem involves *partnership.*

And I will make you a great nation, and I will bless you
and make your name great; and so you shall be a blessing; and I will bless those who bless you, and the one
who curses you I will curse. And in you all the families of
the earth shall be blessed.

God is asking America to partner with Him again, to agree
with His purposes and reasons for establishing this nation. We
need to come into full agreement with the biblical principles
upon which this nation was founded. Since the time of creation,
God has always chosen to work on the earth through people, not
independently of them. If we are to see His purposes accomplished in America, we must partner with Him, allowing Him to
work through us.

Peter Wagner speaks of this partnership with God in history
making:

Our sovereign God has for His own reasons so designed
this world that much of what is truly His will He makes
contingent on the attitudes and actions of human
beings. He allows humans to make decisions that can
influence history.[1]

The third principle associated with Shechem is *responsibility*.
"And the LORD appeared to Abram and said, 'To your descendants I will give this land'" (Gen. 12:7). The word "give" (*nathan*)
not only declares ownership but also means to give a charge, or
*assignment*, as well as giving possession. God was assigning the
land to Abraham and his seed.

God's *gifts* are His *assignments*. My children are gifts, but they
are also very important assignments. If God is calling us to
Shechem, He is certainly saying to us, "I am assigning you the
responsibility of reclaiming this land." The incredible prosperity

of this nation is more than just a gift. It is a very important responsibility from God and an assignment to steward.

At Shechem, *idolatry is cleansed* from the land. In Genesis 35:1-4, after Jacob's encounter with the Lord at Penuel and his peaceful reunion with Esau, Jacob took all of his family and servants to Shechem. He went back to this special place where God had met with Abraham, near where he had laid down his own Jacob nature and built his altar El-Elohe-Israel (God, the God of Israel). And there he commanded his people to bury all of their idols.

If God is calling America to Shechem, which I believe He is, that means He is giving us an opportunity to rid the land of the strongholds of idolatry, such as materialism, pleasure, greed, lust and pride. Just as Jacob went back to his roots—the place where the Lord met with Abraham and promised him the land— God is asking us to go back to our biblical roots in this nation. We MUST bury our idols and return to Him with all our heart.

Finally, in Joshua 20:7, Shechem became one of the *cities of refuge*, places to which those who accidentally took someone's life could flee for protection. It was forbidden for any vengeance to be taken against them while they lived in these towns. According to Hebrews 6:18, the cities of refuge prefigure Christ who became our refuge—"We who have fled for refuge in laying hold of the hope set before us."

In calling America to Shechem, God is expressing His desire to once again become our refuge. He wants to take the places in our nation that are filled with violence, murder, poverty, destruction and fear and turn them into safe havens of peace and refuge.

An article in *National Geographic* several years ago provided a penetrating picture of God's wings. After a forest fire in Yellowstone National Park, forest rangers began their trek up a mountain to assess the inferno's damage. One ranger found a bird literally petrified in ashes, perched statuesquely on the ground at the base of a tree. Somewhat sickened by the eerie sight, he knocked over the bird with a stick. When he gently struck it, three tiny chicks scurried from under their dead mother's wings. The loving mother, keenly aware of impending disaster, had carried her offspring to the base of the tree and had gathered them under her wings, instinctively knowing that the toxic smoke would rise. She could have flown to safety but refused to abandon her babies. When the blaze had arrived and the heat had scorched her small body, the mother had remained steadfast and those under the cover of her wings lived. "He will cover you with his feathers, and under his wings you will find refuge" (Ps. 91:4, *NIV*).

We spoke earlier of the Lord's desire to "visit" us (see Luke 19:44) and the fact that the Greek word actually means "to oversee or shepherd." Like this faithful mother bird, He wants to cover us with His wings, just as He desired to do for Jerusalem. They rejected His offer. I pray that we do not. I desperately want Him as our refuge once more.

Come on, history makers; let's go to Shechem.

# EPOCH-MAKING REVIVAL

If we respond to the current word of the Holy Spirit, becoming a cause-minded, crossing-over people, God will give us a history-making revival in America. One of my favorite verses on revival is Acts 3:19: "Repent therefore and return, that your sins may be wiped away, in order that times of refreshing may come from the presence of the Lord."

As is often the case, our English translation doesn't fully convey the Greek content. The phrase "times of refreshing" is loaded with meaning. "Times" is translated from the word *kairos*, which means "opportune time." Settle it in your thinking once and for all: *Repentance and turning create opportune times for God to move.*

Wuest, a very literal translator of the New Testament, uses the following phrases to translate *kairos*: "epoch-making periods" (see Acts 3:19); "strategic, significant period" (see Acts

12:1); "strategic, epochal time" (see Acts 19:23). Using these definitions, repentance and turning create epoch-making, strategic, significant periods for God to move by His Spirit. I don't know about you, but I'm ready for some "epoch-making" revival. America *must* have one!

## DESIRE A FLOOD OF HISTORIC PROPORTIONS

I looked up the term "epoch making" to make sure I understood it. It means "significant by virtue of ensuing *historical* developments"[1] (emphasis added). I bet you already know I like that "historical" part. Epoch means "a period of time characterized by momentous events or changes"[2] and "a fixed point of time from which succeeding years are numbered."[3]

Now that I've put the dictionaries away and danced around my office for a while . . . that's what we're after! Momentous events and changes. History-making stuff! A revival so great it is historical, one from which succeeding years are numbered. We speak of physical floods this way. The year is remembered, like the Johnstown Flood of 1889 or the Big Thompson Canyon (Colorado) Flood of 1976. The size is measured by how often one of that proportion comes—a 50-year flood or a 100-year flood. We want a flood of the river of God so great that people will speak of it the way they speak of physical floods:

- "Remember the Bangladesh Flood of 1987?"
- "This was a 100-year flood."
- "What a devastating flood!"
- "It changed the very topography of the land."

I want a revival of such monumental proportions that it is epoch making:

- "Remember the flood of God's Spirit in 2001?"
- "It was a 2,000-year flood. There's been nothing like it since Pentecost!"
- "What a devastating flood! It wiped out sin everywhere it went."
- "It changed the very face of America."

Epoch making! Historical!

# BREATHE ON US, O GOD!

The word "refreshing" in Acts 3:19 is important. It is translated from the word *anapsuxis*, from *ana* and *psucho*. *Strong's* says *ana* means "repetition, intensity or reversal."[4] Zodhiates agrees, adding the word "increase."[5]

*Psucho* means "to breathe, blow or refresh with cool air."[6]

Here are some definitions of the two words—*ana* and *psucho*—combined (*anapsucho* or *anapsuxis*):

- "to draw breath again"
- "to revive by fresh air"[7]
- "to cool or refresh with a breath"
- "to regain strength"
- "restoration"[8]

In this verse, Peter is saying that if we respond to the Holy Spirit, it will create a *kairos* time for God to breathe on us again; to revive us with a fresh breath; to restore us, giving us new strength to enable us to draw breath again. *Lord, please do this for America!*

I also like the concept of intensity in *ana*. God wants to breathe on us again *intensely*. That would be epochal! Peter was apparently thinking back a few days to Pentecost—a real epoch-making event—when the breath of God blew again intensely, once more filling humans with the life of God.

In Ezekiel 37:1-14, the dry bones represent spiritual death. First God caused them to come together; then He put skin on them, "but there was no breath in them" (v. 8). The prophet was then told, "Prophesy to the breath . . . say to the breath, 'Thus says the LORD GOD, "Come from the four winds, O breath, and breathe on these slain, that they come to life"'" (v. 9).

This is what happened in Genesis 2:7. God breathed into a lifeless body and brought His life to Adam. Peter thought back through history—Genesis, Ezekiel, Pentecost—and prophesied in Acts 3:19 that it could happen again if the people would obey the Holy Spirit.

It has happened since on numerous occasions:

- in the fourteenth century through John Wycliffe;
- in the fifteenth century through the Lollards movement;
- in the sixteenth century through Martin Luther and John Calvin;
- in the seventeenth century with the Puritan Revival;
- in the eighteenth century through the Wesleys, George Whitefield and others;
- in the nineteenth century as revival swept the United States, Scotland, Wales and England;
- in the twentieth century through the worldwide Pentecostal movement.

God isn't finished, however. He wants to do it yet again! He has another breath—another wind to blow on us. He wants to bring it with great intensity. If we in the American Church will respond to the current word of repentance and cross over, it will create the *kairos*—epoch-making, opportune time—for the Spirit of God to blow on us again. I believe I see it beginning, but it is only in an infancy stage. We must continue the process.

## BUY THE OPPORTUNITY!

When the process of repentance and turning has fully created the *kairos* of *anapsuxis*, we must seize the moment. Twice the New Testament tells us to redeem the time (see Eph. 5:15-17; Col. 4:5, KJV). "To redeem" is translated from *exagorazo*, meaning "buy or purchase," and "time" is from *kairos*—buy the opportune epoch-making time. Buy history!

Opportunities must be bought. They cost something—time, energy, abilities, money, our very lives. If we don't spend what is necessary and buy them, opportunities can also be lost.

When Apple Computer fell on difficult days a while back, Apple's young chairman, Steven Jobs, traveled from the Silicon Valley to New York City. His purpose was to convince Pepsico's John Sculley to move west and run his struggling company.

As the two men overlooked the Manhattan skyline from Sculley's penthouse office, the Pepsi executive started to decline Jobs's offer.

"Financially," Sculley said, "you'd have to give me a million-dollar salary, a million-dollar bonus, and a million-dollar severance."

Flabbergasted, Jobs gulped and agreed—if Sculley would move to California. But Sculley would commit only to being a consultant from New York. At that, Jobs issued a challenge to Sculley: "Do you want to spend the rest of your life selling sugared water, or do you want to change the world?"

In his autobiography *Odyssey*, Sculley admits Jobs's challenge "knocked the wind out of me." He said he'd become so caught up with his future at Pepsi, his pension, and whether his family could adapt to life in California that an opportunity to "change the world" nearly passed him by. Instead, he put his life in perspective and went to Apple.[9]

Let's not miss the opportunity to change our world! Let's buy it!

## SEEK VISION FOR THE HARVEST

Allow God to birth vision in you *now*—vision that will motivate you to faith and action. Vision is a life-changer, a rearranger, a cause producer. Its hunger can be insatiable, a motivating force *creating energy* and *energizing creativity*.

Vision moves us from mere mental assent to physical exertion. It creates history makers. It separates the hearer from the doer, the convert from the disciple, mediocrity from excellence. *It is also what separates a ripe harvest from a reaped harvest* (see Matt. 9:37).

Men give up successful careers due to Holy Spirit

> **Vision is a life-changer, a rearranger, a cause producer.**

generated vision. Some have walked away from great fortune, others from earthly fame as this awesome force of heaven moved into their lives. It messes things up, alters lifestyles, rocks the boat. It rarely goes with the flow—it creates it.

I remember hearing Wayne Myers, a well-known missionary from Mexico, speak in the first missions conference I attended. I was single at the time and still living at home, probably 22 or 23 years old. The first night Wayne ended up with about a third of my bank account for the missions program of the hosting church. The second night he got the next third. You guessed it: The last night he got the rest. If there had been a fourth night, I'd have been walking home—he'd have gotten my car!

There was no manipulation; he didn't *make* me give the money. No one took it from me. What happened? Some of the all-consuming, all-encompassing vision he had for reaching the world with the gospel was imparted to me—that impossible-to-explain, you-just-have-to-experience-it Holy Ghost osmosis that sometimes happens. I've given to missions ever since.

I remember when the vision came to me to reach out to those devastated by pain and suffering. It was 1976, the tenth of February to be exact. The country was Guatemala, the village was San Pedro, the setting was a food line. I was serving soup to hungry women and children who had lost everything the previous week in an earthquake that had killed 30,000 people and left 1 million homeless. I vividly recall dishing out the soup into cans, bottles, jars (whole or broken) and whatever else they could find to hold a little soup. I also remember looking at the last lady in line—a mother holding her two- or three-year-old child who likely hadn't eaten in days—and telling her there was "no more."

Things got all messed up in my life at that moment! I could no longer look the other way and pretend not to see the needs of suffering humanity. I had looked into hungry eyes . . . hopeless eyes . . . haunting eyes. Plans had to be changed; spending habits altered; priorities rearranged. Vision had come to me—I had crossed over. Things have never been quite the same since.

Oh, for eyes NOW to see the potential harvest. For ears to hear the word of the Lord. For insight to understand the times! God is speaking a clear word to those who are listening.

Can you feel the breeze of Pentecost picking up? No, it's not the rushing, mighty wind yet, but the breeze is beginning to blow. I feel it when I pray, worship and commune with Father. I feel it as I traverse this country trumpeting a wake-up call.

I hear the Father asking, "Can these bones live?" (Ezek. 37:3). He is trying to awaken faith in us. If we will only hear and obey, Mr. Wind Himself is about to be unleashed.

I, as Elijah, hear the "sound of abundance of rain" (1 Kings 18:41, *KJV*). The sound isn't yet thunder—don't expect it to be that loud. It is a gentle rumbling in the distance. But it is ominous. It is the voice of the Lord.

*Let the fire fall, Father. Finish Your cleansing work—create a*
*kairos season for the wind. Breathe on us again . . . intensely!*
*May we turn to You with all our heart.*
*Let the rains come. We're dry and thirsty.*
*Let the river flow with great force. Bring a mighty flood! The*
*Flood of 2001—and beyond!*
*In Jesus' name, amen.*

# I WISH I KNEW WHAT I WAS LOOKING FOR

It's difficult to find something when you don't know what you're looking for. I recall the night I sat up late trying to turn off the computer—I never did get it turned off.

I had been playing solitaire. That's all I can do on one of those user-friendly beasts—if someone else turns it on for me, that is. I played till about 11:00 P.M., gave up trying to turn it off about 1:00 A.M. and went to bed.

I had tried everything I could think of, clicked YES to every question except "Do you want to blow up this computer?" I actually said YES to that, too, but backed down when it asked, "Are you sure?"

I thought for a while God might be doing this to me. He's the only one I know who truly has power over computers, and

I've heard He even uses surge protectors. But when the temptation to lose my sanctification became more than I could bear, I knew it wasn't Him. The Bible says He won't do that.

Seated at the breakfast table the next morning, my eyes bloodshot and bags beneath them, Ceci, my wife, looked at me and asked, "Did you sleep okay?"

"Sure," I replied. "Why?"

"Because your eyes look like road maps."

"I was up kinda late," I said, hoping she wouldn't pry for the reason.

"Why?" she pried. (Women are curious, you understand. They need to know these sorts of things. A man wouldn't have cared why.)

"Because I couldn't get the computer turned off," I mumbled.

I saw her and our two daughters glance at each other out of the corners of their eyes. They all had goofy "Did he say what I think he said?" grins. Finally, one of them could contain herself no longer. "What did you say, Dad?"

"I said I couldn't figure out how to turn off the computer," I replied rather sheepishly.

Chuckles, snickers and other unkind noises were my breakfast for the next 10 minutes as I sat thinking of how to get even.

Finally, one of them asked me, "Want to know how to turn it off, Dad?"

"I don't care if I ever find out or not."

"You have to click it to 'start'," she said.

"Right," I replied, "and the earth is flat."

"No," she said, "you really do."

"That's right," Ceci piped up.

"But it was *already* started," I stated.

"I know, but you still have to go to 'start' to turn it off," Ceci said with a smile.

"Why would I start something to turn it off, especially when it's already started?" I asked.

"That's just the way it works," my eight-year-old Hannah said rather condescendingly. "We'll just turn it on and off for you from now on, Dad."

As I said, it's hard to find something when you don't know what you're looking for. One of the reasons we have such a difficult time finding repentance is because *we don't know what we're looking for.* And in our search for revival in America, we must find repentance. Only when the Body of Christ fully comprehends the process of repentance—and lives accordingly—can the river of revival flow through us in its pure state. Anything less causes the waters to be murky, polluted by our flesh, and prohibits crossing over. It is essential that repentance be first worked out in our lives in order for true revival to flow through us and impact the nation.

> **Is our failure to understand repentance the reason we so often "repent" of the same thing again and again?**

## Repentance Means Never Having to Say You're Sorry . . . Again

So what is repentance, anyway? No, it isn't turning from sin and going another way. Nor does it mean remorse or sorrow for that sin. Not that these things aren't *related* to repentance—they are. But to limit our definition of repentance to these is to rob repentance of its incredible power to bring true transformation.

Because we don't really understand repentance, too many Christians repeatedly try to skip the *cause* and go straight to the *effect*. It doesn't work. This is the reason we so often "repent" of the same thing again and again. It's also why only 3 to 5 percent of our converts in America become true followers of Jesus Christ![1]

I intend to teach in this chapter. Let's figure out what we're looking for so we can find it. It is critical that we understand this subject of repentance.

## GOING GOD'S WAY

Properly defining three New Testament words will enable us to understand the process of repentance. These three words are "revelation," "repentance" and "turning."

"Revelation" comes from the Greek word *apokalupsis* and means an "unveiling or uncovering"[2] (from *apo,* meaning "off or away" and *kalupto,* meaning "to cover or veil"). It refers to God lifting the veil from the minds of humans in order to reveal information to them *from a divine perspective.*

"Repentance" is from the word *metanoia* and is literally defined as "knowing after"[3] (from *meta* meaning "after"and *noeo* meaning "to know"). It is a new knowledge, perception or understanding that comes to us "after" our previous understanding. It is a change of mind.

The third word, "turning," is from the word *epistrepho.* It means "to turn" and go a new direction, or "to return."[4] This is the *result* of revelation and repentance. Acts 3:19 says, "Repent, therefore, and return." Notice that repentance (*metanoia*) comes first, then the turning (*epistrepho*).

To better understand this verse, let's paraphrase it, "Repent, *in order that* you can return to God's way." Further clarification might be given by wording it this way: "Get God's knowledge or perspective of the situation—find out what He is saying—so you can turn and go His way."

Let's summarize the three concepts: Man needs an unveiling (revelation) to bring him a new understanding from God's perspective (repentance) so that he can turn and go God's way (turning).

## HUMAN-CENTERED REPENTANCE VERSUS GOD-CENTERED REPENTANCE

A word that looks somewhat similar to the Greek word for repentance, but is very different in meaning, is *metamellomai*. This is what we usually have when we *think* we have true repentance. The word means "regret or remorse."[5] This *pain of mind*, or brokenness, is often the beginning of true repentance, when the consequences of our actions become real to us. Second Corinthians 7:8-11 speaks of this. Nevertheless, it is not yet full repentance and does not produce the desired change. Repentance is a *change* of mind—not just a *pain* of mind—resulting from a revelation brought by God. It is not simply a mental decision based on guilt.

The subtle danger of *metamellomai* is that its remorse is still rooted in *self*—the pain, shame or other negative consequences *I* experience as a result of *my* actions. It could be the loss of *my* family, the loss of *my* ministry, the shame *I* have to endure or even the potential of *my* going to hell if *I* don't change. Zodhiates says it "means little more than a selfish dread of the consequence of what one has done."[6]

The fact that we feel bad about our sin is obviously not the problem. We should feel bad at times. But if it goes no further, feeling bad simply puts us in search of something to remedy *our* pain. This does not get us past the Fall, where humankind became the center of its own universe and its motto in life became "what's in it for ME?" It is, in a very subtle way, still nothing more than humanism, or me-ism. Human-centered repentance makes humankind and its pain or loss the measuring point; true repentance is God-centered.

When the gospel is presented to a sinner, or a believer is repentant of sin, the emphasis should not be upon the person's benefit. This always perverts the outcome. The issue is that we have sinned against a holy God. Nothing and no one else can take center stage, which is why David said when he found true repentance after his sin with Bathsheba, "Against thee, thee only, have I sinned" (Ps. 51:4, *KJV*).

I used to be bothered by this statement—I even disputed it with the Lord. I told Him David had sinned against his wife, the nation Israel, the noble Uriah (Bathsheba's husband and one of David's mighty men) and God. Such an assertion may be accurate in a natural sense, and restitution may be appropriate at times, but that is not the issue where true repentance is concerned. God and God alone is the issue. If this were not so, restitution alone would bring forgiveness from God when we sin against others. Of course, we know it does not. David found true repentance only when he saw his condition from God's perspective and confessed his sin.

Even the "broken and a contrite heart" (Ps. 51:17) that David said pleased the Lord would not have been enough by itself. Many people have a broken or contrite heart yet never come to forgiveness—much less transformation. Judas is probably the best-known example of this. The Bible says he experienced great remorse (*metamellomai*—see Matt. 27:3). He gave the 30 pieces of silver back and hung himself. There is no record, however, of Judas's receiving forgiveness. He didn't find repentance.

Esau couldn't find it either. "He found no place for repentance, though he sought for it with tears" (Heb. 12:17). Again, regret or sorrow is not the same as repentance. And they do not bring forgiveness to us.

> Some years ago a speedboat driver who had survived a racing accident described what had happened. He said he had been at near top speed when his boat veered slightly and hit a wave at a dangerous angle. The combined force of his speed and the size and angle of the wave sent the boat spinning crazily into the air. He was thrown from his seat and propelled deeply into the water—so deep, in fact, that he had no idea which direction the surface was. He had to remain calm and wait for the buoyancy of his life vest to begin pulling him up. Once he discovered which way was up, he could swim for the surface.[7]

If we will wait on Him, God's gentle tug will pull us in the right direction. Our "life vest" may be the Word, another Christian or an inner witness from the Holy Spirit. But the key is to allow Him to show us His way to find repentance.

I refer to repentance as a *process* because it usually comes over a period of time, as we *gradually* are transformed into His way of thinking. In most cases, the course of our ships cannot be changed instantaneously. We aren't made to handle a sudden change of direction; we would capsize. When the unveiling happens and revelation finally breaks in on us, it often seems to have happened suddenly. But in reality, a series of smaller unveilings—increments of truth breaking through, seeds of God's Word being planted—have likely led up to the "sudden" revelation.

Obviously, the larger the ship and the farther off course, the longer the adjustment period. Thus it is often a lengthy process to bring repentance—God's new knowledge or way of thinking—to a nation.

# "PLEASE GO BACK TO YOUR SEAT—YOU'RE NOT READY YET"

Though true repentance and turning bring forgiveness, God's goal is much loftier than this. He's shooting for *transformation*. When we receive revelation from Him, enabling us to see our conditions from His perspective, this unveiling also reveals His grace and redemption to us. We see our need, but we also see His provision. The exposing and humbling of self with the counter-action of God's being exalted allow the release of grace. His grace then empowers and enables us to *effectively* "turn and go the other way."

This is why the great evangelist Charles Finney would often preach four, five or more nights before he gave the first altar call during his crusades. He allowed time for this process of repentance to occur. Finney was actually known to have grown men run to the altar weeping during a message, yet he would tell them, "Please go back to your seat—you're not ready yet." This is also why he had a much higher number of disciples who came out of his crusades than we have today. I have heard figures as high as 97 percent for the number of Finney's converts who became true followers of Christ, and as low as 5 percent for our converts today.

A "What's in it for me?" gospel has taken center stage in our country. This is one of the reasons we're in such a spiritually bankrupt condition. When we preach a humanistic gospel—one that places man at the center—we produce humanistic, self-centered converts. How could a humanistic gospel that never gets self to the Cross, but instead makes the appeal to the self's motivation, do anything else? Preach to people of the blessings, and they love it. Ask for a little sacrifice, and they quickly disappear. Little if anything is said about taking up and living at the Cross *daily*. Most Americans don't even know what it means. "Jesus paid it all, so I can be happy" is really all that matters to them.

Only 3 to 5 percent of the people who donate money to a church actually tithe of their income.[8] Only 60 percent attend a church service weekly. Most never pray or spend time in the Word of God unless *they* need or want something. The average Christian family of four in America today gives $20.80 a year toward foreign missions. The Church of America spends $5 billion annually on new religious buildings, while investing $1 million a year to reach the unreached with the gospel. That's a ratio of 5,000 to 1—buildings over people, comfort over commission.[9] There is very little concern for the cause of Christ.

Discipleship, commitment, selfless giving and living, sacrifice for our commission and other spiritual disciplines don't stand a chance with this anemic gospel. It is costless, causeless Christianity at its worst, and America is inundated with it! God's holy hammer of truth is about to descend on it with incredible force! It would be far wiser for us to fall on the Rock before He falls on us (see Matt. 21:44). We must do it now.

Dr. George Sweeting wrote in *Special Sermons for Special Days*:

Several years ago our family visited Niagara Falls. It was spring, and ice was rushing down the river. As I viewed the large blocks of ice flowing toward the falls, I could see that there were carcasses of dead fish embedded in the ice. Gulls by the score were riding down the river feeding on the fish. As they came to the brink of the falls, their wings would go out, and they would escape from the falls.

I watched one gull which seemed to delay and wondered when it would leave. It was engrossed in the carcass of a fish, and when it finally came to the brink of the falls, out went its powerful wings. The bird flapped and flapped and even lifted the ice out of the water, and I thought it would escape. But it had delayed too long so that its claws had frozen into the ice. The weight of the

ice was too great, and the gull plunged into the abyss. . . .
Oh, the danger of delay![10]

## Transformation Can Only Be Found at the Cross

The irony is that we've taken God's instrument of death for the exalted self-life—the Cross—and made it an instrument of blessing to that life. Our error actually strengthens the problem—the self. God doesn't want to bless self; He wants it dead. One of the greatest heresies we could preach is that Jesus went to the Cross so that we wouldn't have to. This is true in a physical sense but not in a spiritual sense. Jesus actually went to the Cross so that we *could*, bringing the death of the old man. Christ said, "If anyone wishes to come after Me, let him deny himself, and take up his cross daily, and follow Me" (Luke 9:23). The Cross is where we must die *daily*. We have missed this pitifully.

The Cross is not just something to wear around our necks; it is supposed to wear us. Consider the fact that much of the time when Jesus mentioned going to the Cross, He added the fact that we, too, must go there (see Matt. 16:21-26; Mark 8:31-38; Luke 9:22-27; John 12:23-26). More than just a symbolic identification with Him—don't disarm it with such a powerless interpretation—He speaks of a very real laying down of our lives.

When we're told to lay down our *lives* in the New Testament, it is referring to the exalted self-life that came at the Fall. The Greek word used is *psuche*, which is also the word for "soul"—that which contains the mind, emotions and will. Therefore, when we're commanded to lay down our lives, we're being told to lay down the "life" that is rooted in the exalted soul of humankind— that which causes rebellion, independence and self-exaltation. Again, if we don't bring this to the Cross and find true repentance, there will be no transformation.

# "Well, What's the Good News?"

In summary, we have basically missed the mark with our approach to repentance in three ways. First, we have defined it as "turning and going the other way," which jumps to the effect, missing the cause.

Second, we have thought of it as remorse, or being sorry, for our sins. This stops short of true repentance and often focuses the attention back on self, as it seeks to find a way out of its dilemma. Remorse sometimes leads to, and is often the result of, genuine repentance but is not to be confused with it.

Third is the salesman approach—sadly the most destructive—and the area in which we have transgressed the most. We try to "sell" Jesus based on His many wonderful benefits. Perhaps "sell" isn't the best word, because there is certainly no price for the sinner to pay; Jesus paid it all. What remains, then, is for them to cash in on all the benefits. Going to heaven when they die is just the icing on the cake. This is nothing more than an appeal to the exalted self-life, which remains on the throne asking, "What's in it for me?"

Paul said, "My speech and my preaching was not with enticing words" (1 Cor. 2:4, *KJV*). The truth is, we're not salesmen, nor is our gospel some smorgasbord of goodies. Jesus doesn't invite us to "give Me a try." On the contrary, He *commands*: "Take up your cross. Follow Me!"

Our efforts at outreach have become too watered down. This almost always happens during these seasons when God is working more *in* us than *through* us. Because we don't understand the season, we try anything to produce outward growth. Sales and marketing approaches and watered-down gospels become the order of the day—anything to see a little fruit.

When Lloyd C. Douglas, author of *The Robe* and other novels, was a university student, he lived in a boarding house, says Maxie Dunnam in *Jesus' Claims—Our Promises*. Downstairs on the first floor was an elderly, retired music teacher, now infirm and unable to leave the apartment.

Douglas said that every morning they had a ritual they would go through together. He would come down the steps, open the old man's door, and ask, "Well, what's the good news?"

The old man would pick up his tuning fork, tap it on the side of his wheelchair, and say, "That's Middle C! It was middle C yesterday; it will be middle C tomorrow; it will be middle C a thousand years from now. The tenor upstairs sings flat, the piano across the hall is out of tune, but my friend, *that* is middle C!"

The old man had discovered one thing upon which he could depend, one constant reality in his life.[11]

The true gospel message never changes. It included the Cross yesterday; it will include the Cross tomorrow; it will include the Cross a thousand years from now. We may not like it. The world certainly doesn't. But, my friends, the true gospel includes the Cross—our Cross!

In contrast to these false approaches, true biblical repentance—a new knowledge causing us to see our situations from God's perspective—is the result of divine revelation. This breaks the back of exalted self, getting it to the Cross, resulting in transformation and a supernatural ability to turn.

What has this to do with revival and harvest? Everything! The process of revival begins with the process of repentance. And where revival is concerned, it must begin with the Church and then spread to the world. The inpouring *to* us precedes the outpouring *through* us. Revival in the Church will precede revival in the world. He must *revive* us before He can *vive* through us.

God is bringing to us an awareness of our weaknesses, so He can fill them with His strength (see 2 Cor. 12:9). *"He has torn us, but He will heal us"* (Hos. 6:1, emphasis added). He is revealing to us a "new knowledge" in many areas of our lives so we can turn and go His way. The result will be vessels "for honor, sanctified, useful to the Master" (2 Tim. 2:21).

Those who think as He does can be trusted with His gifts and anointings. These blessings will no longer be prostituted for personal gain but will be cast as crowns at His feet. He will increase; we will decrease (see John 3:30). Hebrews think that way. So do cause-minded people.

The result will be life to the world. The *times of refreshing* will come from His presence (see Acts 3:19). The fallow ground will have been broken, righteousness will be rained upon us (see Hos. 10:12), and revival will come.

I'm still looking for that computer switch, but I've found repentance.

## CHAPTER EIGHT

# Not *REALLY* Lost

Have you ever been lost? I have. Well, not *really* lost. I'm a man, you understand. We don't get lost; we simply drive around for hours trying to make others believe we are. It's a game. After a few hours we stop to "use the restroom" and very discreetly check with someone else to confirm that we're not *really* lost.

"Yep, right on target," we declare to our passengers. "All we do is . . ." The most I've not *really* been lost is about 90 miles.

I recall the time I wasn't *really* lost in the woods. I was hunting in an area of Colorado that was new to me. We arrived at our cabin late in the afternoon, and I decided to take advantage of the last couple hours of daylight. *I'll just go scout around a little*, I thought. *This will give me a slight advantage in the morning. And who knows, I might even get lucky and see an elk. Better take my gun.*

I scouted around about 20 minutes too long. This meant a lengthy walk back to the cabin in the dark. No problem. I had my flashlight, compass and survival gear. I wasn't scared. That's why I whistled and hummed as I walked. I always whistle and hum in a woods at night when I'm not *really* lost and not *really* scared.

Somewhere I missed a turn. Things look different going the opposite direction, especially in the dark.

Nothing jump-starts the imagination like being alone and lost—well, not *really* lost—in an unknown woods at night. (Not that I was scared, you understand.) Creatures I don't even believe in live in unknown woods at night. I heard noises that were down-right *weird*. I also walked past approximately 10 mountain lions and 5 bears. Luckily, they heard me whistling, detected my confidence and ran off. It helps to be smarter than they are.

> **Not only do we get off course individually, but movements, organizations and nations do as well.**

In times like these, at some point the mind begins to think crazy thoughts and ask strange questions. *I know all elk are supposed to be vegetarians, but I wonder if some are really meat eaters?* I recall thinking. *They don't have deductive reasoning as we humans, but could they possibly know why I'm out here?*

"Naw!" I heard myself say out loud.

Then for some unknown reason I also heard myself say very loudly, "Sure is a great night for a walk. I hope no elk think I've been hunting them."

Suddenly, something jumped near the trail. Limbs and branches cracked and the ground shook as something sounding like a galloping horse rumbled through the night. After I set a new record for the 400-meter dash, I slowed down to 50 mph and congratulated myself for having the calmness to take advantage of this time alone to enjoy some jogging. If you're going to be *almost* but not *really* lost in the woods, you might as well get in a little aerobic exercise.

"Most guys would never think of that," I bragged to myself. "They'd be too scared." Finally, I came to the main road. I was only a mile or two south of where I wanted to be. *Not bad*, I thought.

As I approached the cabin, my concerned buddies were outside waiting for me. "We were starting to get worried," they said. "Were you lost?"

"Not really," I replied.

"Probably just wanted a little exercise, right?" they remarked in a matter-of-fact manner. Guys understand things like this.

America isn't *really* off course. We're just wandering around exercising in the dark. Yeah, right! The reality of our denial is often lost to us. (Think about that one—it'll come.)

No one is perfect, and all of us have blind spots. We lose our bearings from time to time and need directional adjustments. Not only do we get off course individually, but movements, organizations and nations do as well. We are very human. Someone once said that people are like most folks.

## FIVE WAYS TO GET LOST

We can find examples of movements needing adjustment to God's way of thinking (repentance) in the charismatic and Jesus movements of the '60s and '70s. Because I am a product of these and would be considered a charismatic by many, I can "pick on us" without my comments being of a critical nature. Also, having been a participant, I know them better than I do other movements or organizations.

Here and in the next few chapters, I will discuss five failures which I believe short-circuited these moves of God, causing them to fall short of all He wanted to accomplish through them. Though true of these two movements in particular, these mistakes are common and therefore valid for all movements. My purpose in rehashing these errors is to help us preserve the coming revival and keep it from getting off course.

David the giant killer became a murdering womanizer for a short season. Abraham the Hebrew gave his wife to a king in order to protect himself. Aborted moves of God are as bad as no move at all. We must be alert and aware of these dangers—we must not allow these mistakes to be repeated.

I do not mean to imply that these movements were total failures; though this is a critique of sorts, it is not meant to be critical. God did accomplish much through these particular movements. Through them, thousands were saved and filled with the Holy Spirit; the Jesus movement impacted a very hopeless generation; the teaching office of Ephesians 4:11 was restored to the Church; worship matured immensely and other blessings were released as well. As mentioned, I personally was touched in a major way and am, to one degree or another, a product of these particular renewals.

In spite of the blessings, however, the five weaknesses I want to discuss were very serious. Of course, there may have been more, but these are the ones that stand out in my mind.

## HASTE WITHOUT HEART

The first of these undermining flaws I call *haste without heart*. The biblical passage which illustrates this condition is 2 Samuel 18:19-33. The setting is the death of Absalom, David's son who had stolen the throne from him for a short while.

Then Ahimaaz the son of Zadok said, "Please let me run and bring the king news that the LORD has freed him from the hand of his enemies."

But Joab said to him, "You are not the man to carry news this day, but you shall carry news another day; however, you shall carry no news today *because the king's son is dead.*" Then Joab said to the Cushite, "Go, tell the king what you have seen." So the Cushite bowed to Joab and ran.

Now Ahimaaz the son of Zadok said once more to Joab, "But whatever happens, please let me also run after the Cushite."

And Joab said, "Why would you run, my son, since *you will have no reward for going?*"

"But whatever happens," he said, "I will run."

So he said to him, "Run." Then Ahimaaz ran by way of the plain and passed up the Cushite.

Now David was sitting between the two gates; and the watchman went up to the roof of the gate by the wall, and raised his eyes and looked, and behold, a man running by himself. And the watchman called and told the king. And the king said, "If he is by himself there is good news in his mouth." And he came nearer and nearer.

Then the watchman saw another man running; and the watchman called to the gatekeeper and said, "Behold, another man running by himself."

And the king said, "This one also is bringing good news."

And the watchman said, "I think the running of the first one is like the running of Ahimaaz the son of Zadok."

And the king said, "This is a good man and comes with good news."

And Ahimaaz called and said to the king, "All is well." And he prostrated himself before the king with his face to the ground. And he said, "Blessed is the LORD your God, who has delivered up the men who lifted their hands against my lord the king."

And the king said, "Is it well with the young man Absalom?"

And Ahimaaz answered, "When Joab sent the king's servant, and your servant, I saw a great tumult, but *I did not know* what it was."

Then the king said, "Turn aside and stand here." So he turned aside and stood still.

And behold, the Cushite arrived, and the Cushite said, "Let my lord the king receive good news, for the LORD has freed you this day from the hand of all those who rose up against you."

Then the king said to the Cushite, "Is it well with the young man Absalom?"

And the Cushite answered, "Let the enemies of my lord the king, and all who rise up against you for evil, be as that young man!"

And *the king was deeply moved and went up to the chamber over the gate and wept.* And thus he said as he walked, "O my son Absalom, my son, my son Absalom! Would I had died instead of you, O Absalom, my son, my son!" (emphasis added).

Ahimaaz was very fast. He started last but arrived first. He ran in vain, however—"you will have no reward for going" (v. 22)—because he didn't have the complete message. And he did not have the entire message, because *he didn't identify with the king's heart*. David had not only defeated an enemy, but he had also lost a son. Ahimaaz eventually stepped aside in ignorance, insignificance and embarrassment, as a nameless individual took center stage and delivered the complete message.

*Our message will always in some way be deficient if it isn't related to the King's heart.* I'm speaking, of course, of God our King—our heavenly Father, Jesus and the Holy Spirit. The pleasure of the Father is—and must remain—the ultimate goal of our running. The glory and exaltation of the Son must be our chief aim. His passion and priority of harvesting sons and daughters into the family must become ours.

God is willing now to give His heart for America to those who want it. But beware—His is broken. When He touched my heart with His on October 4, 2000, I wasn't prepared for it. I thought mine would break in two. And now I'm a man with a cause—probably ruined for life. Ask for His heart, but if you do, get ready to change.

### Why Are We Running?

This first problem, haste without heart, begs the question of our *motives* for service. Why are we running? Why are we building, seeking revival? Is it for personal fulfillment, fame, glory, self-aggrandizement, to make a name for ourselves? Or are we, as the Cushite in this passage, content to remain nameless? Is it for advancement, a position? Is it to display our gifts, our speed? Are we looking to build something big?

Still others run for the pure excitement of running. I agree we should enjoy the journey, but we aren't to run for the thrill of it. In Philippians 3:14, Paul said, "I press *toward the mark*"(*KJV*, emphasis added). His goal, or mark as he called it, was clear. In verse 12 (*NASB*), he said, "I press on in order that I may lay hold of that for which also I was laid hold of by Christ Jesus."

### The Gift Mentality

Unfortunately, the charismatic movement, as positive as it was, gave us a *gift mentality*: Run on the strength of your gift. The very word "charismatic" means "grace *gifts*." This led to a *performance mentality*: run to set records, to be first, to be the best, to be the biggest. Go for the gold! "Build 'em big and build 'em fast!" became the mind-set. Overnight sensations were, and in many ways still are, the order of the day. *There is nothing biblical about this mind-set!* Persistent, progressive, hanging-in-there, long-term building should receive more honor than something that springs up quickly. Sadly, it does not. Far more character is needed to build a work or ministry over a long period of time than to enjoy something which happens quickly.

One of the basic problems with this philosophy, aside from its inherent pride and self-exaltation, is that if *any* part of our vision (which becomes the goal of running) is born of *ambition* rather than *God's heart*, we soon are running for *self*, not the King. Zeal that was originally to do something *for God* becomes a zeal *to remain successful*. This change can be so subtle, it frequently happens without our even realizing it. The Church in America is inundated with people who are running for themselves rather than God. That's why no progress has been made in reaching the people of America. The verdict is in.

Contrary to what is often taught—and usually done—*our vision* must never be our starting place. Vision *born of God's heart* must be where we begin. In my younger days it was hammered into me by many: "Get a vision." Again and again, I heard it. They should have been saying, "Find God's heart. Seek His face."

The questions we must continually ask ourselves are, How well do I understand and relate to the King's heart in this matter? Is that and that alone my motive for running, for building? Was His heart the birthplace of my vision?

The question is *not*, How fast or gifted am I? *Never* does this validate our running! God's pattern of service is always in this order:

1. He matures us into His character.
2. He entrusts us with His heart.
3. He directs us with His vision.
4. He enables us with His anointing and provision.
5. He releases us to minister our gifts to accomplish and fulfill His vision.

## Holy Hubert

A gentleman used greatly by God in the early days of the charismatic movement exemplifies a life lived according to God's pattern of service. He was a part of a move of the Holy Spirit that was eventually called the Jesus movement. This movement was used by God to bring thousands of drug-bound, sexually perverted, disillusioned and hopeless young people into the kingdom of God. His name was Hubert Lindsay, but he became known as Holy Hubert. He was a man with a cause!

Like King David, who wasn't called by his father to join the potential king lineup (see 1 Sam. 16), nothing about Holy Hubert's appearance or personality caused him to stand apart. He was short, didn't have much charisma, was even a little "different" from the socially accepted norm.

I once had the privilege of hearing Mr. Lindsay speak. He told of his calling to, and ministry at, the University of California at Berkeley. The people who were there that day may remember what he said about the miracles and the salvations. They may recall the humor with which he spoke—they had laughed, cheered and applauded. What I fear may have been missed, however, was a passing comment Holy Hubert made about how the ministry had been birthed.

"I became so burdened for this generation," he said, "that I would walk the streets of the campus—sometimes all night long—weeping and interceding for those kids. I pled with God to give me those young people." God broke his heart for a generation.

The Lord answered his cry *because it was His own* and gave him a generation. Church historians agree that the Jesus movement was of extreme significance in the renewal of the '60s and '70s. And when tracing the roots of the Jesus movement, one invariably ends up at Berkeley with Holy Hubert Lindsay.

His burden cost him dearly, however. His broken heart led to broken bones—not to a nice salary or a large congregation. Lindsay and his wife were beaten on numerous occasions, stabbed, mocked and ridiculed as they preached the gospel on campus. His wife eventually suffered brain damage, and Holy Hubert lost his sight due to the beatings. Just as the apostle Paul did, they bore on their bodies the marks of the Lord Jesus (see Gal. 6:17).

The Lindsays picture for us the principle of starting, not with a vision, ministry or gifts, but with the heart of God concerning a particular need—and allowing that to become the motivating reason for ministry. This releases revival in a pure form, keeping it free from the debris of pride and selfish motivation.

Our failure to do this resulted in a generation of believers who believed gifting qualifies a person for ministry. We allowed ourselves to bypass character and other heart issues in these movements. God's heart was replaced by other priorities and motivations, which inevitably led us to build our own kingdoms. A cooperative heart (God's) was superseded by a competitive heart (humankind's). Travailing, agonizing prayer was replaced by the strength of our gifts. Last, and probably most tragic, success was measured not by how well we knew the Father but by how well known we were.

Push has come to shove, Ahimaaz has passed the Cushite, and the Father is weeping. Repentance must come. We need an alignment. Our fast-moving state-of-the-art churches are pulling to the right and left. Things are out of balance. We have compensated for our ignorance with speed, and we are out of control.

*Please, Lord, help us see this situation from Your perspective. Give us repentance. We must have an unveiling. Deliver us from ourselves and give us a crossing over that isn't aborted—please!*

## CHAPTER NINE

# Genuine Greatness

In the previous chapter we began to look at key strategies for crossing over without going under. As history makers with a cause, we have a responsibility to prepare for the assignments God is giving us. Let's look at two other weaknesses that derailed the charismatic and Jesus movements and learn how we can avoid these dangers.

## Speed Without Seasoned Skill

The second weakness of these movements, and one to which we are all susceptible, was *speed without seasoned skill*. This is illustrated in 2 Samuel 2:18-23:

Now the three sons of Zeruiah were there, Joab and Abishai and Asahel; and Asahel was as swift-footed as one of the gazelles which is in the field. And Asahel pursued Abner and did not turn to the right or to the left from following Abner.

Then Abner looked behind him and said, "Is that you, Asahel?"

And he answered, "It is I."

So Abner said to him, "Turn to your right or to your left, and take hold of one of the young men for yourself, and take for yourself his spoil."

But Asahel was not willing to turn aside from following him.

And Abner repeated again to Asahel, "Turn aside from following me. Why should I strike you to the ground? How then could I lift up my face to your brother Joab?"

However, he refused to turn aside; therefore Abner struck him in the belly with the butt end of the spear, so that the spear came out at his back. And he fell there and died on the spot. And it came about that all who came to the place where Asahel had fallen and died, stood still."

Though similar to *haste without heart,* this is different. Whereas the first point relates to our *motives,* this weakness speaks of our *maturity levels*: training, preparation, wisdom and understanding. So far as we know, Asahel's motives were fine. He simply didn't have the necessary wisdom for the battle. Ahimaaz ran for the *wrong reasons;* Asahel ran *prematurely.*

A wise person counts the cost before going to war and asks, "Do I have what it requires to win?" Before building, it is prudent to ask, "Do I have the necessary resources to finish this task?"

From New Year's resolutions and our repeated attempts to become more spiritually disciplined to building churches and growing ministries, many of us start projects well but finish poorly. I've seen too many ministries explode quickly into big organizations but eventually fail through compromise or poor planning. It's not how we start the race but how we finish that matters the most.

At 7 P.M. on October 20, 1968, a few thousand spectators remained in the Mexico City Olympic Stadium. It was cool and dark. The last of the marathon runners, each exhausted, were being carried off to first-aid stations. More than an hour earlier, Mamo Wolde of Ethiopia—looking as fresh as when he started the race—crossed the finish line, the winner of the 26-mile, 385-yard event.

As the remaining spectators prepared to leave, those sitting near the marathon gates suddenly heard the sound of sirens and police whistles. All eyes turned to the gate. A lone figure wearing number 36 and the colors of Tanzania entered the stadium. His name was John Stephen Akhwari. He was the last man to finish the marathon. He had fallen during the race and injured his knee and ankle. Now, with his leg bloodied and bandaged, he grimaced with each hobbling step around the 400-meter track.

The spectators rose and applauded him. After crossing the finish line, Akhwari slowly walked off the field. Later, a reporter asked Akhwari the question on everyone's mind: "Why did you continue to race after you were so badly injured?"

He replied, "My country did not send me 7,000 miles to start the race. They sent me 7,000 miles to finish it." [1]

What a wonderful story that powerfully proclaims "Let us run with perseverance the race marked out for us" (Heb. 12:1, *NIV*). God didn't call us to *start* a race—He called us to *finish* it.

In running the spiritual race of life, zeal alone is not enough. Zeal often *generates* but seldom *sustains*. Good intentions are not enough—it's *not* just the thought that counts. Contrary to popular belief, ignorance is not bliss. A great vision, talent, gifts, abilities, speed—none is sufficient for producing the kind of fruit God wants.

The charismatic movement, in spite of its strengths and blessings, in many ways glorified the wrong requirements for our running. Much of the error was directly related to impatience—"now-ism." Speed and gifting, not wisdom and character, were the main criteria for ministry. The following tendencies manifested themselves in the movement and are still alive and well today:

- Knowledge was glorified over wisdom.
- Revelation was exalted over sound doctrine.
- Reaping was given priority over sowing.
- The works of God replaced the ways of God.
- Gifts and charisma took precedence over experience and understanding.
- Instant gratification replaced endurance.
- Formulas and how-tos replaced waiting on God.
- Church-growth and success seminars replaced prayer meetings and prayer watches.
- Seasoning, training and wisdom were neglected for the sake of speed.
- Action took priority over accountability—the ends began to justify the means.
- Fathers without enough fire and speed were rejected—along with their wisdom—and our peers became our

counselors. Fire counseled fire! The results? Fireworks! The problem? After a few bright flashes, it was all over.

Speed and size now spelled success. An instant-gratification, buy-now/pay-later, live-for-today humanistic world somehow succeeded in conforming much of the Church to its ways.

> **Nowhere in Scripture will you find speed or size to be the criteria for success or greatness. I'm not aware of a city in America that has experienced genuine revival as a result of one of the fastest-growing or largest churches.**

Phrases such as "fastest growing" and "one of the largest" became absolute curses to the Body of Christ, curses which continue to operate. Inherent in these phrases are wrong motivation, a deficient understanding of God, the wounding of others and the propagating of a competitive spirit. We not only shoot our wounded in the Body of Christ, but we also often do the wounding with our carnal mind-sets. Nowhere in the Scriptures will you find speed and size to be the criteria for success or greatness, yet they take center stage in our Christian culture. I fear this mind-set has done much more damage than we realize. When our standard of judgment is distorted, the goal invariably goes amiss also.

Enough time has passed that it is now possible to judge the fruit of this distortion of God's ways. *I'm not aware of a city in America that has experienced genuine revival as a result of one of the fastest-growing or largest churches.* In spite of our supposed growth and the many megachurches that now exist, there is not a greater percentage of Americans attending church today than there was 20 years ago. Of the purported growth, 90 percent has been from transfers, not conversions. Unlike His Church, I don't think God is very impressed with our results. He probably spends a great deal of time mourning the Asahels who have been run through with the enemy's spear and grieving over the competitive spirit that permeates the Body of Christ.

I recently read my friend Bart Pierce's book *Seek Our Brothers.* It had a powerful impact on me. Bart pastors a truly great church in Baltimore, Maryland. Rock City Church is great, not because of its size, but because it is truly impacting the city— from the homeless on the street to the business people downtown. In a recent service, Bart mentioned getting over 300 people saved and placing them in another local church (i.e., not his). Now that church is exploding. His explanation: "I don't pastor one congregation; I pastor my city." I didn't know whether to leap and dance or to weep. If all of us could have that heart, we'd have taken America long ago.

We have not understood that the good of the whole is more important than the individual parts. We compete for sheep and choose our leaders based on gifting. Then we wonder why the Body of Christ is in such a mess. Why don't we see more fruit? More people saved? More purity? More depth of commitment? Longer-lasting moves of the Spirit?

Because of our emphasis on speed and size, we have been building without character, without much depth, with a lot of debt and without sufficient foundations to support our structures. We have broken the rules but still want to win the war. But we have not been winning. Instead many, like Asahel, have been speared by the enemy. Casualties abound. And they will continue until we begin to judge by God's standards, not our own.

Let us press on to maturity as we prepare for another wave of revival. Anything less is suicidal.

## Sensationalism Without Substance

The third problem pervading the Jesus and charismatic movements—and, indeed, the Church of today—was *sensationalism without substance*. Revelation 3:1-2 says of the church at Sardis, "You have a name that you are alive, but you are dead. Wake up, and strengthen the things that remain, which were about to die."

This church had obviously been strong at one point and continued to have the reputation of being alive. God, however, looked at the heart of the church and saw its true condition. The fact that these people had a name declaring they were alive tells us they were still "doing the right things." The church looked good, looked alive. In reality, however, it was dead.

The inevitable result of failures, this problem speaks of our *methods*. It represents building, not on the anointing of the Holy Spirit, but on formulas, hype, sensationalism, big names, miracles, the gifts of the Spirit, innovation—anything that breeds excitement. It usually happens because it is *quicker* and *easier* to build this way. *Largeness* is sometimes produced but seldom *longevity*.

Innovation is prioritized over the anointing. Man-made ideas are implemented to achieve production. In our generation, there is no shortage of creative ways to produce revival. Just like King David when he tried to bring the Ark of the Covenant back to Israel, we have produced thousands of "new carts" in our attempts to bring back the glory. They come disguised in many forms, from church-growth seminars to the most innovative and technologically brilliant schemes imaginable. (And I might add, many of them are inspired with good motives.) E. M. Bounds said it well: "We are constantly on a stretch, if not a strain, to devise new methods, new plans, new organizations to advance the Church and secure enlargement and efficiency for the gospel."[2]

I sometimes hear talk of mighty meetings but find only hype and sensationalism when I arrive. I hear words like "impact" and "change" but see very little of it after the meetings. I heard of one well-known evangelistic team's great crusade a few years back where more than 2,000 young people were supposedly won to Christ in a single week; yet a few months later I could find only one convert in an area local church. Revival? I don't think so.

This weakness results in what I term "placebo Christianity." The outside looks good, but the inside lacks substance. It looks alive, but it is dead. Perhaps most alarming is that placebo Christianity standardizes mediocrity. The Church of America now has this disease.

## The Samson Effect

An overemphasis on power, miracles and emotional stirrings always leads to sensationalism and, ultimately, a *decrease* in power. Like the church at Sardis, the life and anointing of the Holy Spirit die while the reputation of the church lives on. Don't forget, has-beens used to be. As with Samson, this can take place without our even being aware of it. "'I will go out as at other times and shake myself free.' But he did not know that the LORD had departed from him" (Judg. 16:20).

This pattern inevitably leads to cynicism on the part of the world and disillusionment in the Church, two conditions prevalent today. I have watched several churches and ministries built this way: Excitement prevailed, Christians transferred, and these works became the latest "fastest-growing, cutting-edge, overnight sensations." The magazines came, articles were written, television shows were produced, and money was made. Many of these churches and ministries are now dead or mortally wounded.

Others still have a name that they're alive but are basically dead. None have taken cities. Heaven weeps while we go do the same thing somewhere else—create another overnight sensation and play our Kingdom success games.

And what is the fruit? Our cities and nation are no different—no, that's not really true. They are much worse! Generation X still waits for something real. Christians grow more disillusioned, the world more cynical.

I will know that this perversion of truth has been broken off the Church in America when church janitors, long-term Sunday School teachers, no-name intercessors, nursery workers and any number of other good and faithful servants make the cover of our magazines and are interviewed on our television programs— when we begin to judge the way heaven judges, when we glorify what God glorifies! When I see loyalty lauded over transiency, faithfulness over flashiness, consistency over charisma and substance over sensation, I'll know things are changing. "Too strong, Dutch" you say? Not as strong as the Bible. Jesus said our lukewarmness makes Him want to throw up (see Rev. 3:16).

## Genuine Greatness

I don't think we understand greatness at all. Most of us will be totally confused at the awards ceremony in heaven. I can assure you of this: It won't look like ours. I have some truly great people in my fellowship. You won't hear of most of them until we get to heaven. They're not "gifted" enough. They're simply great moms and dads, great workers, great servants.

My grandfather Bill Henkel died recently. He was almost 90. He didn't leave me a penny. It wasn't there to leave. He lived in a small house in a small town. He never preached a sermon, but his life continues to speak. So does his seed. Known for his integrity, my grandfather's handshake and his word were enough for anyone who knew him, *including his bank*. My brother once saw him get a loan at the bank without even a signature! He was truly humble. When he was saved, he crawled to the altar. He was in church every Sunday and most Wednesdays, and he served in various capacities. He tithed and gave to many needy people, though he had to work two and sometimes three jobs to survive. He only had an elementary education, yet his children love God and his grandchildren preach the gospel.

*He was a great man!* Heaven celebrated his arrival. I wept and rejoiced at the legacy he left me, worth far more than money.

Understanding sensation and hype better than we in the Church do, the world is crying out for some substance from us "God-people." We will never reach them using their own methods. A capitalistic, may-the-best-man-win world is waiting to see some true love—giving, sacrificial, preferring one another, unconditional *agape*.

A proud, be-the-best, claw-your-way-to-the-top generation would be defenseless in the face of genuine humility and servanthood.

A people who created the hydrogen bomb and went to the moon but can't control their own flesh or keep a family together, would be immeasurably impacted by a display of true inner strength.

A race so desperate for the supernatural that it will embrace almost any new weird religion or psychic would bow the knee if the true and living God were allowed to answer by fire, working some genuine miracles in their midst.

Let's shake off the shackles of perverted theology and its dead religion! Let's raise the standard back to the biblical level. Let's not be merely human, let's be Christ-ians—little Christs.

Let's insist on the real thing. Let's cross over . . . make some history.

God and the world are waiting.

## CHAPTER TEN

# POURING A SLAB AND THROWING A PARTY

Having now discussed three weaknesses of the charismatic and Jesus movements, weaknesses which still exist in much of the Body of Christ, we now want to look at the fourth pitfall. Again, my purpose is not to criticize but to help us to avoid repeating the mistakes of the past.

As the river of God continues to rise, we want to ensure that it flows unabated. We desire to obey Hebrews 12:1: "Lay aside every encumbrance, and the sin which so easily entangles us, and let us run with endurance the race that is set before us."

To assist us, our loving Father is bringing revelation, repentance and turning. He is disciplining us, not out of cruelty or a punishing motivation, but to bring an increase of "the peaceful fruit of righteousness" (Heb. 12:11). He is training us to be history makers, Hebrews at heart.

The word "trained" in Hebrews 12:11 is from the Greek word *gumnazo*. We also get the word "gymnasium" from it. God is taking us to the gym for some spiritual fitness exercise. He wants us to win the race. He's a great trainer and a loving Father. We can trust Him. We must remember this as we look at our weaknesses.

## REJOICING WITHOUT REFLECTING, MERRIMENT WITHOUT MOURNING

The fourth of these past and present weaknesses—*rejoicing without reflecting, merriment without mourning*—is illustrated in an interesting passage of Scripture, Ezra 3:10-13:

> Now when the builders had laid the foundation of the temple of the LORD, the priests stood in their apparel with trumpets, and the Levites, the sons of Asaph, with cymbals, to praise the LORD according to the directions of King David of Israel. And they sang, praising and giving thanks to the LORD, saying, "For He is good, for His lovingkindness is upon Israel forever."
>
> And all the people *shouted with a great shout* when they praised the LORD because the foundation of the house of the LORD was laid. Yet many of the priests and Levites and heads of fathers' households, the old men who had seen the first temple, *wept with a loud voice* when the foundation of this house was laid before their eyes, while many shouted aloud for joy; so that the people could not distinguish the sound of the shout of joy from the sound of the weeping of the people, for the people

shouted with a loud shout, and the sound was heard far away (emphasis added).

As the book of Ezra opens, Cyrus, king of Persia, has allowed a remnant of Israelites to return to Jerusalem for the purpose of rebuilding the Temple. Seventy years prior, the people of Israel, because of their apostasy, had been taken into captivity by Nebuchadnezzar, king of Babylon. They came under the rule of Cyrus when he conquered Babylon. God then moved the heart of Cyrus, an idolatrous king, to allow the Israelites to return to Jerusalem, and even stirred his spirit to help them raise the needed funds (see Ezra 1:1-4).

Wicked, ungodly politicians are not the main problem in America, contrary to what most of the Church believes. God is capable of dealing with them—one way or another. When He doesn't, we need to ask why.

A remnant of Israelites had returned to their homeland under the leadership of Zerubbabel, and work on the Temple had begun. The celebration we read of took place after they had laid the foundation.

Notice the contrasts in the Ezra passage above. Some were rejoicing so loudly they were heard far away. Others, such as the old men who had seen the first Temple, were weeping with a loud voice. It must have been quite an event to witness.

We are not told why the older ones were weeping. Perhaps because the restoration was beginning, or maybe they were remembering the pain of the captivity with its tragic loss. They could have been reflecting on the former glory of the Temple and thinking how far away they were from its full restoration. They might have even been lamenting the apostasy that created its destruction. We are never told the reason. I think a good guess would be all of the above. One thing is certain: They had a different outlook. While many were laughing, these men were crying.

The problem with this fourth weakness has to do with our *perspective*, our need for a balanced approach to life and ministry. We need a proper mix of tears and laughter, fun and work, joy and mourning.

Fraiser of Lisuland in northern Burma translated the Scriptures into the Lisu language and then left a young fellow with the task of teaching the people to read.

When he returned six months later, he found three students and the teacher seated around a table, with the Scriptures opened in front of the teacher. When the students each read, they left the Bible where it was. The man on the left read it sideways, the man on the right read it sideways but from the other side, and the man across from the teacher read it upside down. Since they always occupied the same chairs, that's how each had learned to read, and that's how each thought the language was written.

We, too, can be like that. When we see something from only one perspective, we may think it's the only perspective. Sometimes it's good to change seats to assume a different perspective on the same truth.[1]

Too little rejoicing makes us dull and religious. It results in oppression, legalism, the destruction of zeal and vision, and the sapping of strength and vigor. The joy of the Lord is our strength (see Neh. 8:10). Lack of it makes our message terribly unappealing. You've probably heard of the sour-faced Christian who approached the wino with the invitation to go to church with him. Taking a long look at him, the wino replied, "No thanks. I have problems enough of my own."

Nothing in the passage from Eza suggests that the rejoicing of the people was improper. In fact, the opposite seems true—it was a good thing. And it is for us as well.

## Premature Celebration

On the other hand, too much rejoicing can result in our losing sight of the essentials, such as our cause and the condition of the world. This is precisely what happened to these Israelites. They poured a slab and threw a party. Shortly thereafter, however, they abandoned the rebuilding process for 16 years. The love of pleasure and ease can rob us of our willingness to work, sacrifice and "endure hardship as a good soldier" (2 Tim. 2:3, *NKJV*).

The Israelites abandoned their work because of fear, discouragement, political pressure (see Ezra 4:4-5) and selfishness (see Hag. 1:1-12). Other people in the area, who didn't want the Temple rebuilt, hired political lobbyists to work against the Israelites, spreading rumors of rebellion to the king; and eventually the intimidation accomplished its goal. By the time the mortar of the foundation set up, fear and discouragement set in.

They used the excuse that it wasn't yet God's *opportune time* (Hebrew word *eth*—see Hag. 1:2) for the Temple to be restored. After all, they reasoned, there wouldn't be all this opposition if it really was God's opportune time. So the building of the Temple stopped for 16 years—all they had was a party slab. Then they conveniently decided it *was* time for them to build their own homes and businesses. To turn them to repentance, God raised up the prophet Haggai to warn them of their deception.

"Consider your ways!" he cried.

> "Is it time for you yourselves to dwell in your paneled houses while this house lies desolate?" Now therefore, thus says the LORD of hosts, "Consider your ways! You have sown much, but harvest little; you eat, but there is not enough to be satisfied; you drink, but there is not enough to become drunk; you put on clothing, but no one is warm enough; and he who earns, earns wages to put into a purse with holes" (Hag. 1:4-6).

This description of the lack of fruitfulness in Israel describes America, including the Church of America. We produce more than any other nation, but it isn't enough—our greed is insatiable. Despite our wealth, our debt is overwhelming. The land of the free is now the home of the bound.

And what of the Church? Much home building has gone on, but it hasn't been His. The Church, whose heritage is to be the lender (see Deut. 28:12), probably spends more annually in interest to banks than it does to evangelize the world. We have done less with more than any other generation of believers in Church history. Our greatest growth of late has been that of our debt and apathy. And as with the Israelites of Ezra's time, discouragement and fear are now prevalent for many of the same reasons: our own failures and seeming lack of fruitfulness, the attack and ridicule of the world, and the overall state of affairs in the earth.

*"Consider your ways!"* is a word to us today. It is time to stop doing our own thing, building our own kingdoms and seeking our own gain. It is time to build the Lord's house! *It is the opportune time!* He who changes the times and seasons is doing it again (see Dan. 2:21). My prayer is that the age of apathy toward God's agenda comes to a screeching halt—that God pulls the legs out from under our easy chairs.

In Haggai's day, the message had its desired effect. Biblical repentance occurred—revelation, repentance (a new understanding) and turning God's way. Work on the Temple resumed and so did God's favor and blessing. He eliminated the political pressure, removed the influence of the lobbyists and brought restoration.

Can He do this today? Absolutely! When we respond to Him, as these Israelites did, He will once again bless our labors as He did theirs, and we will see there is no longer any basis for our discouragement and fears. We are not at the mercy of the politicians and evil lobbyists in our nation's capital. They can't stop revival, as long as we obey the Lord. God never predicated revival on what they do. He can *move* the heart of the king (politicians) or *remove* him. Revival is determined by us. "If *my* people, which are called by my name, shall humble themselves, and pray, and seek my face, and turn from their wicked ways; then will I hear from heaven, and will forgive their sin, and will heal their land" (2 Chron. 7:14, *KJV*, emphasis added).

As a character in the comic strip "Pogo" said, "We have met the enemy, and he is us."

## Blessed Are Those Who Mourn

Sometimes we, as these Israelites, allow our partying to be premature. It is so much easier and fun to party than to work. And celebrating is certainly more fulfilling than mourning.

The pain on the earth—hunger, war, poverty, abuse, rape, the sufferings of the spiritually lost—is often too depressing to think about. Sometimes I want to silence the Mother Teresas of the world. I want to rejoice so loudly that I can't hear their tears. They rain on my spiritual parade.

Somehow, we must learn to rejoice over our successes and the good things of life without being blinded or intoxicated by them. Our ostrich eyes are caked with mud and sand. We must be able to enjoy the goodness of our God and the joy of our salvation without its anesthetizing us to the pain around us and the fact that billions still haven't heard the good news. Somehow, we must marry the two. "Jesus . . . for the *joy* set before Him *endured* the cross, despising the *shame*" (Hebrews 12:2, emphasis added).

We must allow ourselves to be touched by the pain around us. Our Father does. He'll watch every one of the 4,000 abortions in America today. With the broken heart of a loving Creator, He'll reread the plans He had written for them in His book of destinies (see Ps. 139:16). He'll weep over the millions of fatherless children searching for identity. His heart will break as the stomachs of the hungry ache with need. He is looking for someone to share His pain. Are we too busy partying?

Merriment without mourning created a lot of trouble in the charismatic movement. We didn't know how to mourn. We lost the ability to weep. I have been rebuked by pastors for trying to awaken people to the pain and need of humanity. These pastors didn't like sending their members home unhappy, spoiling their Sunday dinners. They might have left and gone to another fellowship where they could hear what they wanted and party on.

Remember the story of Holy Hubert (in chapter 8)? As the crowd listened to the testimony of Holy Hubert, I recall how we clapped about what he wept to get. It seemed a bit unfair to me. I couldn't help but reflect on how easy it was for us—and how costly for him.

> **Somehow, we must be able to enjoy the goodness of our God and the joy of our salvation without its anesthetizing us to the pain around us and the fact that billions still haven't heard the good news.**

In my early days participating in the movement, I remember disliking and turning off to those who had genuine burdens from the Lord. I wanted to laugh, dance, rejoice and confess the blessings of the Lord, not be knocked off my "high" by someone with a burden. Heaven must have wept as we laughed.

The Holy Spirit tried to get our attention through some fathers who had enough wisdom to see what we couldn't. One of them was a man named Charles Duncombe. Brother D, as so many called him, was older—a wealth of wisdom, very sensitive to the Holy Spirit—and considered a true father in the Lord by many. Also being a great and eloquent speaker, he was in much demand.

In the early '80s, however, he brought a warning to the charismatic movement. Seeing the shallowness and deception of much that was happening, especially the inward focus and the "bless me" mind-set that had set in, he tried his best to sound the alarm.

Was he listened to? Far from it—it was party time! He was ostracized by the Body of Christ. By the time he died, Brother D couldn't get a meeting. People didn't want to hear the warning. Most of us were too blinded by our celebrations to see the reality of the situation.

He wrote a powerful booklet entitled *Blessed Are Those Who Mourn,* trying once again to awaken us. He could find no one who would even consider publishing it. It was too confrontive, offensive, controversial, alarming, noncharismatic. It wouldn't have sold well and, after all, prosperity *was* the bottom line. So they published more books on how to prosper and succeed—Christian "Think and Grow Rich" stuff.

He gave the manuscript to me shortly before he died, saying, "You can have it; no one else wants it." To this day it sits on my bookcase, screaming its indictment against us. We're listening now—the party's over. And I'm weeping as I write.

On the last page of the booklet, Brother Duncombe said, "I mourn because the great charismatic move of the last few decades is not headed for revival."

The verdict is in. We produced growth, not disciples. We prospered greatly and focused it all inward. Our liberty in the spirit became license. Our newfound independence from traditions and dead forms turned to independent spirits.

And God turned away.

The movement died, a season of correction came, and now, in His sovereign wisdom and great mercy, God is bringing forth another season of restoration. Will it become revival in America as it has in other parts of the world? It can and I pray it will. If it is going to happen, however, we're going to need a little more mourning, sowing the precious tear seeds spoken of in Psalm 126. *Then* we can rejoice, bringing in the sheaves of harvest.

## CHAPTER ELEVEN

# PREPARING THE WAY

The last of the five pitfalls that short-circuited these movements—*Elishas without Elijahs,* sons without fathers, ministers without mentors—speaks of the need we all have for spiritual fathers in our lives.

Let me say from the beginning, when I speak of spiritual fathers and sons, I am not referring to gender. I am speaking of function. Women certainly can and do fulfill the biblical criteria for sonship and fathering, in the same way we men are a part of the Bride of Christ. We are speaking of the relational aspect and the need it fulfills, not the particular gender.

There came a point in my walk when I recognized my great need and found myself asking, almost in a murmuring way, "Where have all the fathers gone?" Sometime later I realized what had happened to many of them—they were run over and trampled by us young zealots.

They didn't have the speed, muscle and fire that we Ahimaazes and Asahels had (see chapter 9); and rather than honoring their experience and wisdom, allowing them to father us, we pulled "an Absalom." We cast them aside, took their pulpits and/or members and "showed them how to do it."

We were teenagers showing the fathers how to run. And run we did—into buildings, trees, pits and anything else in our way. We never did find the finish line, but we arrived there first! God is still cleaning up the mess.

## WHERE ARE THE FATHERS?

I am not a Church historian, but I cannot imagine a movement in Church history that placed so many novices in ministry positions. Why did it happen? Because of our emphasis on speed, size and gifting. A few years down the road, with our churches struggling, our members disillusioned and the world laughing, we began to cry out for fathers.

Some of them are cautiously beginning to rise from the rubble of rejection and wonder if there really is a place for them after all. Others who have experienced the frustration of being fatherless (though perhaps self-inflicted) have allowed the Lord to develop them and bring them into fatherhood. Thank God He is raising up spiritual fathers.

I spoke to the spiritual father of a well-known minister a few years back, sharing concerns I saw in this minister's life and ministry. The father agreed.

"Why don't you do something?" I asked.

"He no longer listens to me," the father answered with obvious concern. "He's too big, too popular, too important."

It should come as no surprise that this young man has since been publicly exposed for his lack of integrity in ministry.

Never outgrow your need for Dad! What happens when we do? What did our independence produce in the charismatic movement?

- Leaders who produce action without accountability
- *Works*-oriented ministries that don't know the *ways* of God
- Lording leaders who haven't learned to lead by serving
- The prostituting of gifts for gain
- Leaders who know how to birth children but not how to train and nurture sons and daughters

## The Fruits of Spiritual Fatherhood

If we allow them to, what will spiritual fathers teach and produce in us?

- Seeing the subtleties of pride and selfish ambition, they teach us humility.
- Recognizing the danger of isolation and one-person shows, they teach us dependence—our need for one another.
- Understanding the seasons of the Spirit, they teach us patience—the ability to wait.
- Knowing you can't build on miracles, sensation and the works of God, they teach us the ways of God and the principles of His Word.
- Knowing the strength and subtlety of sin, they demonstrate the need for accountability and provide it.
- Helping us become fathers, they prevent the next generation from being spiritually illegitimate.
- They remove the curse from the land (see Mal. 4:6).

- They prevent haste without heart, speed without seasoned skill, sensationalism without substance and rejoicing without reflecting, thereby preserving the flow of revival.

It is no accident that the Scriptures say the young men see *visions*, the old men dream *dreams* (see Joel 2:28). One possible interpretation of this is that vision points ahead, while literal dreams are born of things we have seen or experienced in our past. One causes us to run *aggressively* (vision), the other with *perspective* (dreams). When the foundation for the Temple was poured, the visionaries partied and the dreamers wept. Both are essential!

## THE CLEANSING POWER OF THE RIVER

In order to correct these five weaknesses in the Church, God has begun a work of cleansing: revelation, repentance and turning. The depth of the river diminished to a trickle as He exposed sin, flesh, carnality, wrong motives and unscriptural ways. He loves us too much to allow our weaknesses to rob us of our destinies; He loves the lost too much to allow our weaknesses to rob them of His river. So the correction continues.

John the Baptist paved the way for the new and greater anointing in his day. "Clear the way" is the action foretold of him in Isaiah 40:3. "Then the glory of the LORD will be revealed," verse 5 continues. The way must be prepared for God's glory—renewal, restoration, revival, awakenings, crossing over. Isaiah said the valleys, mountains, rough ground and rugged terrain must all be cleared into a highway.

I term this the "bulldozer anointing." When a road is being built, it gets very messy before it gets nice. Mud, holes, metal rods, heavy equipment, sloppy concrete, roadblocks and detours are part of the process of building a road. We tolerate it, however, because we envision a nice, new, smooth road to travel.

God begins the passage in Isaiah 40 by saying, "Comfort, O comfort My people" (v. 1). He then describes and prophesies the bulldozer anointing of John the Baptist. John's message went something like this, "Repent, you bunch of snakes" (see Matt. 3:7-8).

Comfort?

Yes, comfort. The comfort isn't in the process—the clearing, bulldozing and repenting. The comfort is the end result. A highway is prepared for God. A place to cross over. The glory can come. The ministry of Jesus can flow to and through us.

God is too just and kind to bless us in our sin. And His glory is too strong, consuming sin and idols. If He did not do a work of cleansing before sending it, His glory would devastate us.

John the Baptist's bulldozing message was one of repentance. That *is* the message of road building—way building—and it results in the ability to turn His way. Foretelling the ministry of John, an angel said:

> And he will *turn* back many of the sons of Israel to the Lord their God. And it is he who will go as a forerunner before Him in the spirit and power of Elijah, to *turn* the hearts of the fathers back to the children, and the disobedient to the attitude of the righteous; so as to *make ready* a people prepared for the Lord (Luke 1:16-17, emphasis added).

Christ could then follow him with the greater anointing, bringing deliverance and God's favor and glory. Not in the wilderness, but in the Hebrew land of inheritance.

## AMERICA, STRENGTHEN THE THINGS THAT REMAIN

The Church of America has been in the wilderness. In the '80s God began this work of cleansing in the Church. Many people called it a shaking, and a shaking it was (see Heb. 12:25-29; Hag. 2:6-7). God began a ruthless work of exposing sin, impure motives and carnal ways in the American church. Some blamed it on the devil, but it was God.

I don't think He is finished. Too much sin, compromise, apathy and lukewarm living lingers in us. There has been change but not enough. Most of our optimism in this land is nothing more than denial.

We are like the boy who was trying out for a part in the school play. He had his heart set on being in it, and his mother was concerned he would not be chosen. On the day the parts were announced, the boy rushed up to his mother, eyes shining with pride and excitement. "Guess what, Mom," he shouted. "I've been chosen to clap and cheer."[1]

That's good denial; ours isn't. We seem to think we are the only empire that can never become a has-been. America continues to lose ground to sin and perversion. In a recent survey, 70 percent of Americans essentially said it made no difference to them if their president were an adul-

> **The prayer movement, the men's movement, unity, youth breakthroughs, renewal—all these indicate things are changing. Perhaps the most encouraging thing of all is that the Holy Spirit continues to cleanse and awaken.**

terer. As long as prosperity and a strong economy exist, they wanted him left alone. A recent issue of our local paper carried an editorial titled, "If Times Are Good, That's All That Matters."[2] We are a nation on a collision course with judgment. And for the most part, believers are sleeping through it.

We are a religious nation, not a godly nation. Jesus denounced the Pharisees as "whitewashed tombs" (Matt. 23:27). We are much the same. We look good outwardly, but the stench of death is inside. We say, as did the church at Laodicea, "I am rich . . . and have need of nothing" (Rev. 3:17).

To this the Lord says:

> You do not know that you are wretched and miserable and poor and blind and naked. I advise you to buy from Me gold refined by fire, that you may become rich, and white garments, that you may clothe yourself, and that the shame of your nakedness may not be revealed; and eyesalve to anoint your eyes, that you may see. Those whom I love, I reprove and discipline; be zealous therefore, and repent (Rev. 3:17-19).

His admonition to Sardis is also appropriate:

> Wake up, and strengthen the things that remain, which were about to die; for I have not found your deeds completed in the sight of My God (Rev. 3:2).

As stated earlier, it would be a dangerous deception to blame America's problems on the unsaved. We, the salt and light of God, have allowed much of our nation's decay through our prayerlessness and compromise. We have lowered the standard. And so the discipline of the Father continues.

It is not too late. There are signs of hope. The prayer movement, the men's movement, unity, youth breakthroughs, renewal—all these indicate things are changing. Perhaps the most encouraging sign of all is that the Holy Spirit continues to cleanse and awaken.

Will this wilderness season bring the needed correction or at least change it to the point that revival can come? Does turning back to God bring revival, or does revival bring the turning? Both. If enough people hear what God is saying, repent and turn to Him, God will bring the river of His Spirit to us in such a way that others will be swept in. They will then be touched by the fire and cleansing of the Lord.

It is time we return to Him with all of our heart, with fasting, weeping and mourning, rending our hearts and not our garments (see Joel 2:12,13). "Who knows whether He will not turn and relent, and leave a blessing behind Him" (v. 14).

Thank God, to correct our deficiencies He has initiated another time of cleansing and the *process* of revival has begun. We have been through shakings. We've gone into the wilderness. We have visited Hebrews 12—Dad is showing us we're not fatherless and we are loved. The Cross is being resurrected. (How's that for an oxymoron?)

Hallelujah! The *process* of repentance has begun the *process* of revival. The river can and will flow in increasingly deeper levels if we cooperate with the Holy Spirit.

We, the Church, can either stumble our way through this wilderness process and hope that we will eventually cross the Jordan into our destined purpose; or with understanding we can follow the cloud as it leads us through the preparatory dealings of God and get on with the business of moving into the new. The wilderness is NOT our destiny. Canaan—where we possess our inheritance, eat the fruit of our salvation and function in our God-ordained role as "the light of the world" (Matt. 5:14)—is our destiny!

No more denial! Don't stay on the sidelines clapping and cheering. You have a part to play, history maker.

Yes, there is a cause.

# ENDNOTES

## Chapter 1

1. *Twenty-Six Translations of the Bible* (Atlanta, GA: Mathis Publishers, 1985), p. 939.
2. Peter Marshall and David Manuel, *The Light and the Glory* (Grand Rapids, MI: Fleming H. Revell, 1977), p. 271.
3. Tom Brokaw, *The Greatest Generation* (New York: Random House, 1998), p. 18.
4. Statistics by the U.S. Youth Risk Behavior Surveillance, 1995, U.S. Dept. of Health and Human Services Public Health Service Centers for Disease Control and Prevention, Atlanta, GA 30333; http://users.chartertn.net/kabennett/rt/rtstat.htm (accessed August 28, 2001).
5. U.S. Dept. of Justice, Special Report, September 1988; http://www.fathermag.com/news/1780_stats.shtm/ (accessed August 28, 2001).
6. George Barna, *Boiling Point* (Ventura, CA: Regal Books, 2001), p. 93.
7. George Barna research study, March 8, 1999.
8. Barna, *Boiling Point*, p. 213.
9. Ibid., p. 191.
10. Ibid.
11. George Barna's surveys do not specifically ask people to identify themselves as "born again." The "born again" percentages are based on responses to questions such as, "Have you ever made a personal commitment to Jesus Christ that is still important in your life today?" and a response such as, "After I die, I know I will go to heaven because I have confessed my sins and have accepted Jesus Christ as my Savior."
12. Barna, *Boiling Point*, p. 189.
13. Ibid., p. 91.
14. Ibid., p. 80.
15. Craig Brian Larson, *Illustrations for Preaching and Teaching* (Grand Rapids, MI: Baker Books, 1993), p. 123.
16. Patrick Henry, "Give Me Liberty or Give Me Death," March 23, 1775. *The University of Oklahoma Law Center*. http://www.law.ou.ed (accessed July 4, 2001).
17. George W. Bush, quoted in Iain Lemos, ed., *Celebrating America's Spirit Together: The 54th Presidential Inauguration* (n.p.: Epicenter Communications, Inc., 2001), p. 4.

## Chapter 2

1. *USA Today,* 1999.
2. Peter Marshall and David Manuel, *The Light and the Glory* (Grand Rapids, MI: Fleming H. Revell, 1977), p. 307.
3. Ibid., p. 309.
4. Ibid., pp. 284-285.
5. http://www.bartleby.com/124/pres13.html (accessed August 21, 2001).
6. Marshall and Manuel, *The Light and the Glory*, pp. 285-286.
7. Ibid., pp. 310-311.
8. Ibid., p. 312.
9. *USA Today*.
10. Martin Smith, "History Maker" (UK: Curious? Music, 1998).

## Chapter 3

1. Strategic, opportune time.
2. Craig Brian Larson, *Illustrations for Preaching and Teaching* (Grand Rapids, MI: Baker Books, 1993), p. 21.
3. James Strong, *The New Strong's Exhaustive Concordance of the Bible, Hebrew and Chaldee Dictionary,* ref. no. 5680.
4. Ibid., ref. no. 5674.
5. Spiros Zodhiates, *The Complete Word Study Dictionary* (Iowa Falls, IA: Word Bible Publishers, 1992), p. 1756.
6. Ibid.
7. Strong, *The New Strong's Exhaustive Concordance,* ref. no. 5676.
8. Ibid., ref. no. 3772 (cf. Zodhiates, p. 1737).

## Chapter 4

1. *Universal Subject Guide to the Bible* (Nashville, TN: Royal Publishers, 1965), p. 91.
2. The teaching in this paragraph was shared by Chuck Pierce at Springs Harvest Fellowship, Colorado Springs, Colorado, on March 4, 2001.

## Chapter 5

1. C. Peter Wagner, *Confronting the Powers* (Ventura, CA: Regal Books, 1996), p. 242.

## Chapter 6

1. *New Webster's Dictionary and Thesaurus of the English Language,* s.v. "epoch making."

2. Ibid.

3. *The Consolidated-Webster Encyclopedic Dictionary*, s.v. "epoch."

4. James Strong, *The New Strong's Exhaustive Concordance of the Bible* (Nashville, TN: Thomas Nelson Publishers, 1990), ref. no. 303.

5. Spiros Zodhiates, *Hebrew-Greek Key Study Bible—New American Standard*, rev. ed. (Chattanooga, TN: AMG Publishers, 1990), p. 1804.

6. Spiros Zodhiates, *The Complete Word Study Dictionary* (Iowa Falls, IA: Word Bible Publishers, 1992), p. 1496.

7. Ethelbert Bullinger, *A Critical Lexicon and Concordance to the English and Greek New Testament* (Grand Rapids, MI: Zondervan Publishing House, 1975), p. 631.

8. Geoffrey W. Bromiley, *Theological Dictionary of the New Testament*, abridged (Grand Rapids, MI: Eerdmans, 1985), p. 1352.

9. Craig Brian Larson, *Illustrations for Preaching and Teaching* (Grand Rapids, MI: Baker Books, 1993), p. 278.

## Chapter 7

1. These figures were given to me in 1984 at Christ for the Nations Institute. I cannot imagine they have changed much since that time, since no greater percentage of Americans attends church regularly now than at that time.

2. Spiros Zodhiates, *Hebrew-Greek Key Study Bible—New American Standard*, rev. ed. (Chattanooga, TN: AMG Publishers, 1990), p. 1809.

3. Ibid., p. 1856.

4. Ibid., p. 1834.

5. Zodhiates, *Hebrew-Greek Key Study Bible*, p. 1856.

6. Ibid., p. 1856.

7. Craig Brian Larson, *Illustrations for Preaching and Teaching* (Grand Rapids, MI: Baker Books, 1993), p. 174.

8. George Barna, *How to Increase Giving in Your Church* (Ventura, CA: Regal Books, 1997), p. 20.

9. David Barrett, *Our Globe and How to Reach It* (Birmingham, AL: New Hope Publishing, 1991), n.p.

10. Larson, *Illustrations for Preaching and Teaching*, p. 180.

11. Ibid., p. 27.

## Chapter 9

1. Edward K. Rowell, *Fresh Illustrations for Preaching and Teaching* (Grand Rapids, MI: Baker Books, 1997), p. 71.

2. E. M. Bounds, *Power Through Prayer* (Grand Rapids, MI: Baker Book House, 1977), p. 5.

## Chapter 10

1. Craig Brian Larson, *Illustrations for Preaching and Teaching* (Grand Rapids, MI: Baker Books, 1993), p. 179.

## Chapter 11

1. Jack Canfield and Mark Victor Hansen, *A Third Serving of Chicken Soup for the Soul* (Deerfield Beach, FL: Health Communications, Inc., 1996), p. 239.
2. Mike Barnicle, "Commentary," *(Colorado Springs) Gazette,* February 16, 1998, news section, p. 5.

*For information about other resources*
*by Dutch Sheets, call or write:*

DUTCH SHEETS MINISTRIES
1015 GARDEN OF THE GODS
COLORADO SPRINGS, CO 80907
PHONE (719) 548-8226

*Or visit Dutch Sheets Ministries online at:*
www.dutchsheets.org

# Best-Sellers from Regal

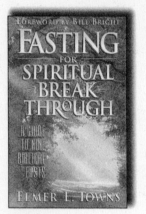

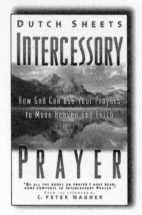

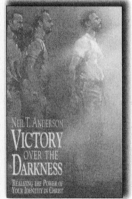
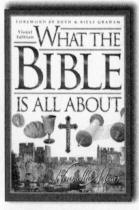